AF632436

Methods of Teaching
CIVICS

Methods of Teaching
CIVICS

Dr. T. Shankar

Crescent
CRESCENT
PUBLISHING CORPORATION

[The responsibility for the facts stated, conclusions reached and plagiarism, if any, in this book is entirely that of the Author. And the Publisher bears no responsibility for them, whatsoever.]

Methods of Teaching Civics

© Reserved

Edition : 2026

ISBN : 81-8342-064-8

Published By :
CRESCENT PUBLISHING CORPORATION
4806/24, Mathur Lane,
Ansari Road, Darya Ganj,
New Delhi - 110002
Mob. : +91-9711991838, 9999021668
Ph. : 011-23244131
e-mail : crescentbook@gmail.com

Website : www.crescentpublishingcorp.weebly.com

Laser Typesetting by :
Adee Computers

Printed at :
Balaji Digital
Delhi

Preface

Civics is the science of comparative government and means of administering public trusts—the theory of governance as applied to state institutions. It is usually considered a branch of applied ethics and is certainly part of politics. Within any given political tradition or ethical tradition, civics refers to education in the obligations and the rights of the citizen under that tradition. When these change, so often does the definition of civics. Related education in history, religion and media literacy is often included.

Civics education is learning for effective participation in democratic and development processes at both local and national levels. It is an important means for capacity development on the societal level by empowering people for effective civic engagement. It is an essential dimension in strengthening a society's ability to manage its own affairs and is complementary to capacity development on the individual and institutional levels. At the core of civics education are the values and principles of transparency, participation, responsiveness, accountability, empowerment and equity.

This book contains highly useful information on diverse core issues of civics with special emphasis on teaching aspect of the subject. It covers a range of innovative teaching techniques aimed at engaging students in the learning processes. It will help teachers of civics to be creative and imaginative in the way they teach the subject.

Dr. T. Shankar

Contents

1

Civic Education

Civic Education is a critical and effective empowerment tool for promoting citizen participation in democratic and development processes. It empowers citizens, both as individuals and as part of collective groupings. Citizen participation is built by protecting individual and collective rights and ensuring appreciation of each citizen's obligations to the society of which s/he is a part. Civic Education can also play a significant role in reducing poverty and achieving the MDGs. Civic Education is generally understood to comprise three elements: civic disposition, civic knowledge and civic skills.

Civic disposition involves citizens:

- Developing confidence to be able to participate in civic life
- Participating in civic life
- Assuming the roles, rights and responsibilities usually associated with citizenship in democratic systems
- Being open, tolerant and responsible in exercising their rights and responsibilities

Civic knowledge means citizens:

- Understand their political and civic context
- Know their social and economic rights as well as their political and civil rights
- Understand the roles, rights and responsibilities of citizenship

Civic skills involve citizens:

- Acquiring the ability to explain, analyse, interact, evaluate, defend a position, and monitor processes and outcomes
- Using knowledge for informed participation in civic and political processes

There are a number of pre-conditions for effective Civic Education. Chief among these is the willingness of government to facilitate discussion of and act upon the issues likely to arise from Civic Education interventions. It is important that government is seen not just as one of a number of potential partners but as the pivotal actor, the disposition of which will have a major impact on the ability of Civic Education programmes to function and produce results.

Other pre-conditions for effective Civic Education include:

- Ensuring that necessary rights of assembly, expression, association and others are recognised and protected
- Active interest from a variety of stakeholders, particularly civil society
- Provision of resources to enable longer-term Civic Education initiatives to be undertaken

Civic Education is essential for sustained poverty reduction and can make a substantial contribution towards the achievement of the Millennium Development Goals (MDGs) which are: It is not just developing and developed country governments and their partners, such as UNDP and others, that need to work to achieve the MDGs. The contribution of people and their "creative energies" is also essential. Civic Education is a critical people-centred tool for liberating these creative energies.

The crucially important role of Civic Education is recognised in many of UNDP's Democratic Governance Practice Notes. It is also emphasised in UNDP's second Multi Year Funding Framework (MYFF), 2004 – 20074, and is an important building block in all the MYFF core goals.

Civic Education and civic engagement are not one and the same. Civic engagement is stimulated, enhanced and deepened through Civic Education, that is, by developing the civic disposition, civic knowledge and civic skills of citizens. Civic Education is thus a mechanism for civic engagement. Civic engagement entails several interrelated but distinct processes. These include people being involved in decision-making, participating and contributing to development and political processes, and sharing in the benefits from these processes. Service learning (learning while involved in some kind of community service) and civic volunteering are two forms of civic engagement that contribute to greater participatory democracy and strengthening civic community.

Creating space and opportunities for voluntary action, especially for national volunteers in areas ranging from supporting people living with HIV/AIDS to electoral assistance and humanitarian relief, makes an important contribution to more cohesive societies by building trust and reciprocity among citizens.

Civic Education for All

All citizens—male and female; young and old; civil servants; politicians; rural or urban—can benefit from Civic Education programmes. A reinforcement of civic disposition, civic skills and an enhancement of the knowledge base of all citizens can make a significant contribution to achieving development objectives. For example, in an electoral context a voter education campaign should ensure that all voters are made aware of and understand their rights and responsibilities.

Education for the Poor

In keeping with the Millennium Declaration and UNDP's mandate in this regard, it is clear that particular concern and emphasis be placed on those who are poor and marginalised. This will require the development of targeted initiatives designed to ensure the empowerment of these groups and to resist the danger of capture of participation opportunities by powerful interests that may arise prior to or following Civic Education programmes. In particular these initiatives will need to take as their starting point the realities of those who are poor. For example:

- Low levels of literacy.
- Apathy, cynicism and distrust in the goals and intent of Civic Education programmes—due to years of oppression, exploitation and marginalisation.
- Perception of risk—there may be reluctance to discuss, let alone speak out on issues of concern. Time and the involvement of acceptable intermediaries will be key in establishing and building trust.
- More pressing priorities—for some, Civic Education may appear to be an unaffordable and irrelevant

luxury in the midst of a daily struggle for survival. Setting aside sufficient time to participate in Civic Education activities in the context of these pressing priorities will be a challenge, particularly for women. Specific efforts will be needed to ensure that the relevance of Civic Education to improving living conditions is clear and that activities are organised to meet the needs of the target community, not the organising entity.

If pro-poor outcomes are to be realised, Civic Education must be seen within the context of achieving broader equity within society. Government in particular will need to be committed to this and to ensure that political space is afforded to enable this to happen. It will also need to be committed to responding to the concerns of the people, particularly poorer groups in society. A key challenge is to recognise that existing power structures and centres within a particular society may be inherently opposed to pro-poor development. In fact, they may actively resist the change that can result from empowerment through Civic Education. Governments and other groups that control power and resources need to understand the different and sometimes competing sets of priorities in society and ensure that the concerns of the poor are taken account of.

Gender Equity and Civic Education

Civic Education programmes offer valuable opportunities both to enhance women's participation in development and governance processes and to address issues of gender equity at national, regional and local levels. However, there is some evidence that general Civic Education programmes can have a more beneficial impact on male participants, increasing their potential for civic engagement more so than for women. Research carried out by USAID on adult Civic

Education programmes in a number of countries suggests that: "Men tended to receive greater benefit from Civic Education than women and that, while women showed gains in a number of important areas, Civic Education tended to reinforce gender disparities in the political realm." General Civic Education programmes and/or programmes specifically designed for working with men/boys should therefore actively address issues of gender equity, reinforcing the reality that gender equity is not just an issue for women and/or women's organisations.

Understanding Civic Education Needs

Before considering involvement in Civic Education programmes and prior to any programme design it is essential that country offices have a good understanding of Civic Education needs and what is being done to address these needs. This can be done by undertaking a situation analysis. Key points to keep in mind in carrying out a situation analysis for Civic Education include:

- Recognise that effective Civic Education takes time, especially in pre-conflict and post-conflict situations.
- Identify existing key actors that are promoting areas of civic knowledge, enhancing specific civic skills and inculcating civic disposition (e.g. government/state agencies; CSOs; the media; private sector groups; political parties; donors; resource organisations (in country or regionally) and others.
- Identify existing government policies/statements on Civic Education.
- Clarify the constitutional and/or legal framework within which Civic Education programming might

take place and identify relevant treaty and legislative obligations assumed by the State.

– Map existing Civic Education provision by identifying thematic areas addressed, target groups, sectoral priorities (formal/informal), geographical scope, methodologies used, materials availability, partnerships and linkages, and the level of existing Civic Education capacity.

An outline of some of the key issues that should be addressed in carrying out a situation analysis, such as the need to map the communication and information needs of marginalised groups. Based on the above and in conjunction with all relevant stakeholders, an assessment should be made of the existing Civic Education landscape. This will identify gaps in existing provision, prioritise areas of unmet needs, and confirm UNDP's specific niche for work in this area. The niche area is likely to reflect UNDP's:

– Commitment to empowering poor people and to citizen participation

– Strong capacity to link Civic Education with broader governance and poverty reduction agendas and to make linkages across a range of other priority human development areas

– Effective relationships with key Civic Education partners, especially host governments and CSOs, and an ability to foster good working partnerships

– Ability to link into regional and global networks and to draw on existing organisational policy and practice

Civic education can be

– Issue based—focusing on a particular topic such as HIV/AIDS or perhaps an environmental issue

- Oriented towards particular groups such as women, youth etc., with a view to addressing particular issues or raising political participation
- Event specific—for example Civic Education linked with an election process
- Implemented at national, regional or local levels
- Formal or informal—targeted on the formal school system or focused on informal, community-based structures

There are a number of ways in which UNDP can engage in Civic Education. These can be broadly grouped into thematic options and modality options. Identified below are six illustrative examples. Three represent possible programming modalities for Civic Education and three illustrate possible thematic linkages with Civic Education.

Voter and Civic Education

Voter and Civic Education are amongst the most commonly requested and potentially influential areas of UNDP's electoral assistance activities. However, Civic Education requirements do not begin or end with elections and in fact need to continue for a longer period. Planning a Civic Education component within an electoral assistance process requires consideration of a number of important factors.

- Voter education is just one component of a broader Civic Education approach (rather than the other way around). As such it should ideally not be carried out in isolation from broader civic education campaigns, though this sometimes happens in practice. One consequence of focusing on more limited voter education activities may be a population that has some understanding of an election process but has little real understanding of where it all fits within the larger democracy canvas.

- Adequate time is essential to develop Civic Education programmes – preferably one year in advance of an election to begin development and implementation of Civic Education interventions. This ensures that appropriate messages can be developed, repeat opportunities for learning and discussion created and understanding supported in a meaningful and sustainable fashion.
- Adequate time is especially essential in post-conflict situations for ensuring that capacity development needs (of CSOs, government, media, private sector) are identified and addressed.
- Early thinking on and planning for the post-electoral situation is essential, even though often the primary focus of voter and Civic Education in an electoral context may be on the elections. Without this, gains made in the run up to and during the elections can be eroded in the vitally important post-electoral period.
- Programming for longer-term Civic Education within an electoral context has implications for project/ programme design options. Direct electoral support may only require a relatively short project period while Civic Education programmes inevitably require a considerably longer period.

Conflict Prevention

For most countries the experience of long or short-term crises, either naturally occurring or man-made, can severely undermine democratic governance and with it, the capacity or willingness of citizens to enjoy their rights or meet their responsibilities as citizens. Civic Education processes can play an important part in crisis/conflict prevention, conflict resolution and crisis/conflict recovery through:

- Restoring belief in the value of peaceful resolution of conflict, reconciliation, tolerance, mutual respect etc.
- Recognising the central role of information provision and the creation of dialogue opportunities in peace-building strategies.
- Supporting early efforts to focus on citizen empowerment and selfreliance thereby countering the potential creation of a dependency culture in post-crisis recovery situations.
- Helping to prevent or lessen the potential for natural disasters and to heighten readiness if they do occur.
- Raising awareness on the role of women in crisis recovery.
- Enabling specialised capacity development to be undertaken in areas such as mediation, conflict transformation, community development and others.

The seriousness of the HIV/AIDS crisis and UNDP's role in tackling it has been well documented in the 2002 Policy Note on HIV/AIDS and Poverty Reduction Strategies and in the Fact Sheet on UNDP's Role in Response to HIV/AIDS. One of the key messages from both of these documents is the clear need for UNDP to contribute to creating an enabling environment "focused on helping developing country governments meet the tremendous governance challenges posed by the epidemic". To do this three core areas for UNDP involvement are identified: Leadership and Capacity Development; Strategic Planning and Implementation; and Advocacy and Communication.

It is principally, though not exclusively, within the last of these that Civic Education initiatives can play a major role. This could be done by:

- Including a focus on HIV/AIDS as one thematic area within a broader Civic Education programme.
- Producing education materials that clearly establish the link between the HIV/AIDS epidemic and broader development and governance issues and which counter discrimination against people living with HIV/AIDS.
- Supporting specific HIV/AIDS Civic Education campaigns.
- Focusing on the most marginalised groups to ensure that lack of education and information does not increase their vulnerability.
- Ensuring a strong focus on capacity development for awareness raising and communication around the issue, especially amongst marginalised groups.

Civic Education Project

This option maintains an individual project approach while ensuring that stronger and more structured linkages are made with other projects/programmes. It offers a number of clear advantages:

- A clear and prominent focus on one or more of the core elements of Civic Education that communicates an important signal of support to and interest in Civic Education programming
- Facilitation of practical linkages and integration across a range of MYFF goals

- Potential to develop partnerships and management structures, specifically around Civic Education
- Greater clarity of content and approach which may appeal to some donors with a specific interest in Civic Education
- Potential for a more manageable vehicle for operational partnerships and cooperation with other UN Agencies, and in the process mobilise more significant resources for Civic Education activities
- Potential to create a strong staffing resource to support and advise Civic Education components in other programmes

A number of country offices have moved towards the development of multisectoral programming, especially in the Democratic Governance area. In several cases, including Tanzania, Fiji, Lesotho and Sierra Leone, Civic Education features prominently. The multisector approach has particular advantages:

- Strong design connections can be established between distinct sectoral activities. For example, programmes on citizenship rights and responsibilities could be more closely integrated with parliamentary accountability processes or with efforts to promote civic engagement or civil society strengthening.
- Learning synergies may be facilitated as a result of a multisectoral approach. A Civic Education component running alongside a programme to reform public administration offers the project management team an enhanced insight into how more effective mechanisms can be created that encourage stronger civic engagement and participation. It can also offer a

framework in which to introduce and test such mechanisms.

- Significant economies in the operation of programme management structures. Opportunities for partnership building between Government and CSOs present themselves in the management structures of multisectoral programmes

Operationalising Inter-project Civic Education Linkages

This option ensures that a Civic Education dimension is included at the design stage of all Democratic Governance programmes. Creating appropriate linkage mechanisms to ensure synergies between different Civic Education activities, and allocating specific staffing resources to coordinate and optimise those linkages would be important for maximising the effectiveness of this option. This option offers the following advantages:

- It is an effective alternative option for situations in which country offices may not have the resources to pursue the dedicated Civic Education and the multisectoral programming options
- It has the potential to deepen the level of involvement and commitment of existing partners
- It has the potential to optimise resource sharing as inter-project linkages supporting Civic Education are strengthened
- It enables cost sharing to support capacity development for Civic Education

There are a number of factors that will influence how the country office decides to engage in Civic Education. These include:

1. *The attitude and outlook of government*: In some cases governments will be keen to develop Civic Education initiatives. In others, the interests of different national stakeholders may face government resistance, if not outright hostility. In some instances in the past, lack of respect for the political sensitivities, the existing power structures and cultural specifics of a nation in the design and implementation of Civic Education programmes has fuelled suspicion of Civic Education processes. The key learning from this is the need to grow Civic Education programmes slowly and carefully and to maximise the use of existing knowledge and resources. Where examples or packages are taken from outside, careful adaptation is essential. In the development of efforts to introduce dedicated or cross-sectoral Civic Education projects this will inevitably prove to be one of the most important issues to be addressed.

2. *The outlook of other project partners*: How willing are CSOs, the private sector and other project partners to work with UNDP on Civic Education issues? In most cases there would appear to be a very strong willingness. However, using CSOs as an example, it is important to consider the lessons of past years of engagement with CSOs, which emphasise that relationships be built on the basis of real partnership, not merely to serve project or programme needs. The Policy Note on Engagement with Civil Society provides valuable advice in this regard.

3. *Existing capacity*: Is there an already existing base of Civic Education activity in the country and has it produced experienced trainers, facilitators, materials producers, etc? This will play a big part in the selection

not only of the most appropriate engagement option but also in the scale of activity to be considered.

4. *Timing*: Timing is a key factor. If a country office is in the early stages of a Common Country Assessment (CCA) process or in the development of the UNDAF, the potential for the creation of dedicated Civic Education programmes or of cross-sectoral programmes is greater. However, if a country office is in mid-cycle, with an existing range of projects/ programmes already in operation, then efforts to build in a Civic Education dimension as part of a programme/project review process may be a more realistic proposition. Inevitably this will involve negotiation with the relevant project partners.

5. *Time availability*: The time available for Civic Education activities to be designed and implemented is also an important factor. If there is a long time horizon available, evidently there is more scope for situation analysis, detailed design, partnership building and sustainable implementation of activities. If sufficient time is not available, then the scale of Civic Education intervention will need to be tailored to maximise results.

6. *Resources*: Resources of course will be one of the most important determining factors. In a situation of abundant resources and strong donor interest in Civic Education, there will be capacity to develop dedicated projects or multisectoral initiatives. Similarly in many of the specific contexts illustrated it is likely that related funding options will exist. However, while resources are important, it should also be remembered that considerable progress can be made by refocusing existing resources and by combining the efforts of existing projects or programmes.

It may be the case that a combination of options will be most appropriate. For example, in a cross-sectoral governance programme in a post-conflict scenario, a Civic Education component with a strong peace-building dimension would suggest itself. Similarly a longer-term programme to strengthen electoral management capacity could facilitate the introduction of a Civic Education programme focusing on citizenship rights, roles and responsibilities.

Capacity Development

Capacity development plays a crucial role in enabling people to exercise their rights. For example, developing people's capacities to communicate, organise, analyse, negotiate and to take a position on a range of issues. Developing the capacities of staff in key government institutions and other powerful organisations is equally important. Capacity development is therefore at the heart of all three components of Civic Education: civic disposition, civic knowledge and civic skills:

Civic disposition	*Civic knowledge*	*Civic skills*
– Developing confidence to be able to participate in civic life – Participating in civic life – Assuming the roles, rights and responsibilities usually associated with citizenship in democratic systems – Being open, tolerant and responsible in exercising their rights and responsibilities	– Understanding their political and civic context Knowing their political and civil rights as well as their social and economic rights – Understanding the roles, rights and responsibilities of citizenship.	– Developing the ability to explain, analyse, evaluate, and defend a position – Using knowledge for informed participation in civic and political processes

Capacity development for Civic Education requires that existing capacities are identified, acknowledged and used, and that the process of developing and implementing Civic Education programmes is recognised as capacity building in itself. The authors of Capacity Development: New Solutions to Old Problems cite two "mistaken assumptions" to be at the root of previous approaches. The first mistaken assumption is to "ignore existing capacities in developing countries and replace them with knowledge and systems produced elsewhere—a form of development displacement rather than development as transformation". The second is that donors can "control the process and yet consider the recipients to be equal partners".

Monitoring and Evaluation Methodology

A key challenge for UNDP supported Civic Education initiatives is to establish a monitoring and evaluation methodology that will identify changes which occur or seem likely to have occurred in levels of civic knowledge, skills and/or civic disposition. A number of key points should be remembered:

- Set clear objectives.
- Ensure that monitoring and evaluation systems, including impact assessment indicators, are agreed with communities and other partners and introduced in the early stages of project/programme development.
- Work to ensure broad stakeholder ownership and management of the monitoring and evaluation systems. The processes are less likely to be effective if they are seen as being externally imposed or just serving the reporting needs of donors. Ownership is also aided by an emphasis on participatory methods, especially those that take literacy issues into account.

– Manage carefully all aspects of the involvement of external "experts".

– Be aware of the need for participants to see and value the benefits of conducting impact assessment. Otherwise there is a real danger of simply adding another evaluation burden onto communities, with no corresponding reward.

– Ensure that a commitment to learning and practice improvement guides the process.

– Ensure that there is a mix of qualitative and quantitative information.

– Participant and community based information provision and analysis is hugely important but its reliability needs to be tested and balanced with external input.

– Commit to viewing the monitoring and assessment process as part of Civic Education, ensuring that the learning that results benefits not just funding agencies but participants within Civic Education programmes.

Building Partnership

Building partnerships for development in any sector is a complex process. Those for Civic Education throw up their own specific challenges. The country context and the particular nature of the Civic Education intervention will influence the composition of any partnership arrangement. For example, if the focus of a Civic Education intervention is to build the confidence of poor people to participate in local events, UNDP may want to involve both local government and CSOs as partners. Strategically important actors for Civic Education include:

- The host government and state institutions
- Civil society (including CBOs, NGOs, education institutions/ organisations, faith-based groups, women and youth groups)
- The media
- Political parties
- The private sector
- Other UN and multilateral organisations

While there is no set formula for partnerships, there are a number of critical components which can contribute in varying degrees to a successful partnership. These include:

- Clear criteria for identifying relevant partners
- Mutual trust and commitment
- Well thought-out project plan with clear objectives
- Responsibilities and roles of each partner clearly defined
- Transparency on each partner's expectations from the partnership
- Ongoing monitoring of the relationships within the partnership

UNDP—Government Partnerships

As UNDP's principal partner, host governments, state institutions including the legislature and judiciary are central to any discussion of Civic Education partnership. However, it is by no means certain that governments or their institutions will always be willing or able to support Civic Education initiatives. The Tanzanian case study illustrated earlier provides an example of a situation where a government policy framework established a strong basis for a partnership with UNDP and civil society, to develop not only Civic Education and civil society strengthening options, but also to integrate these with other aspects of governance development. However, not all contexts will be as conducive as this one. The following factors will influence the extent to which UNDP can progress Civic Education:

- Civic Education may not be a government priority in the context of immediate poverty concerns
- There may be limited recognition or understanding of the role Civic Education can have in supporting development objectives
- The existence of a political system or culture that is hostile to Civic Education (i.e. Civic Education is perceived as threatening or as interference in decision-making)
- Reluctance on the part of government to work with other partners, especially civil society.
- Absence of an obvious government partner where Civic Education effectively runs across a range of ministries and agencies.

UNDP—Civil Society Partnerships

The ability of many CSOs to work with communities at different levels, particularly with grassroots communities, means that partnerships with the civil society sector are crucial for Civic Education programmes. CSO involvement in the implementation of Civic Education programmes is relatively widespread. However, it is increasingly recognised that they also need to be more involved in project design and management. The following factors are important considerations in UNDP's partnerships with civil society:

– The nature of the relationship between government and civil society. In some national contexts the relationship between civil society and the government may be open and receptive but in some countries it may be hostile. Partnerships around Civic Education may be a valuable forum to resolve tensions.

– The involvement of a range of CSOs needs careful consideration. Different CSOs possess different attributes and capacities. It is widely agreed that partnership should not be limited to NGOs alone. Cooperation with CBOs, such as farmers groups or water user groups and mass organisations such as women's organisations, faith-based groups and trade unions may also be necessary.

– The need to recognise and understand the existing capacity (and limitations) of those CSOs working to further democratic governance and development.

– Education institutions/organisations are likely to be of particular importance given their potential contribution to providing or developing Civic Education capacity.

UNDP—Media Partnerships

The media is an important shaper of public opinion and has the potential to contribute significantly to the effectiveness of Civic Education programmes. The importance of an independent, neutral, pluralist, professional and socially responsible media for improving governance and poverty reduction efforts cannot be understated. National, local and community media play an important information intermediary role, mediating information flows between the public, government, the private sector and UN agencies. The following factors are important considerations in UNDP's partnerships with the media:

- Existing capacity of media organisations and their staff. In many cases this may be limited and staff may not be sufficiently skilled to develop and/or produce Civic Education messages.
- The balance between commercial and community media. Community-based/owned media are a very powerful tool but may suffer from resource and capacity constraints.
- The degree to which different media entities reach or are capable of reaching out to marginalised communities.
- Geographical coverage and communication infrastructure. Both may be limited in many countries and will inevitably be stronger in urban centres.
- Literacy levels are fundamental in Civic Education programming and can be a significant barrier if not addressed appropriately. It is therefore important to identify and support media outlets that are able to communicate to those that are not literate (e.g. community radio, street theatre, drama groups, etc.).
- Political orientation and support for democratic values. Some media entities may be directly linked with political parties and while this does not exclude partnerships it signals the need for caution to ensure that progressive Civic Education rather than political objectives are being served.

UNDP—Political Party Partnerships

Political parties are central actors in processes to promote progressive civic values and in increasing civic knowledge. They are by nature influential, highly visible and are often organised down to grassroots level. In addition, they frequently possess the capacity to shape (positively and negatively) public perceptions on key issues. Much of UNDP's work with political parties to date has been done in the context of support for parliamentary development and in election related programmes. The following factors are important considerations in UNDP's partnerships with political parties.

- UNDP will need to strike a balance between the partisan interests of government and opposition parties in all Civic Education work. Transparency and trust are central factors.
- Engagement with political parties within Civic Education programmes can make a significant contribution to the creation and acceptance of a political culture based on democratic values.
- Involving political parties can lead to a broader appreciation by citizens of participatory democracy processes outside of more traditional forms of representative democracy.

UNDP—Private Sector Partnerships

Corporate Social Responsibility (CSR) is an increasing priority of the private sector. It is a term more often associated with global level partnerships, but is one equally suited for application at national and local levels. There is a growing realisation amongst some multinational and indigenous companies that in addition to achieving their commercial objectives, more could be done by the private sector towards achieving the MDGs and consolidating democracy. Civic Education has an important role to play in enhancing transparency and accountability mechanisms within the private sector and in the fight against corruption.

An important consideration in UNDP's partnerships with private sector organisations is to recognise that the private sector can play many diverse roles. For example, resourcing Civic Education initiatives (media campaigns, production of materials), and providing a work environment in which employees are able to take part in political processes (time, and freedom from political discrimination).

UNDP—UN Family Partnerships

Civic Education is an area of activity that lends itself well to interagency partnerships, given the shared interests by many different UN Agencies in democratic governance, in the education sector, in crisis prevention and recovery and other areas. Some of the UN agencies that are actively engaged in Civic Education include: United Nations Volunteers (UNV), UNESCO, UNICEF and UNAIDS. In its role as the UN Resident Co-ordinator, UNDP has the potential to take the lead in promoting a more strategic UN-wide approach to Civic Education. One of the key challenges is to enhance collaboration within the UN Development Assistance Framework (UNDAF) to promote and deepen Civic Education.

2

Methods of Teaching Civics

Citizenship has meant involvement in public affairs by those who had the rights of citizens: to take part in public debate and, directly or indirectly, in shaping the laws and decisions of a state. In modern times, however, democratic ideas led to constant demands to broaden the franchise from a narrow citizen class of the educated and the property owners, to achieve female emancipation, to lower the voting age, to achieve freedom of the press and to open up the processes of government. We now have the opportunity for a highly educated 'citizen democracy'. With the rise of nation states there developed a secondary sense of citizenship: people who, even in autocratic states, had the protection of the laws—such as they were—and the duty of obeying them.

In the nineteenth century, for instance, to say that someone was a Russian citizen or an American citizen meant something very different. The 'good subject' and the 'good citizen' meant different things. In Britain, there was often a problem of perception over this distinction. The very continuity of our history, powers being handed down to Parliament by the Crown in response to gradual pressure from below, has made the very concept of 'British subject' and 'British citizen' seem much the same to most people. Recently the terms 'good citizen' and 'active citizen' have come back into currency.

The report of the Commission on Citizenship, appointed by the then Speaker of the House of Commons, Encouraging Citizenship, did well to adopt as a starting point the understanding of citizenship found in the late T.H. Marshall's book, Citizenship. He saw three elements: the civil, the political and the social. Discussing the first element, the commission rightly put greater stress on the reciprocity between rights and duties; and, more than Marshall, on welfare being not just provision by the state but also what people can do for each other in voluntary groups and organisations, whether local or national. Both of these it saw as a duty it called 'active citizenship', but it had less to say about Marshall's second element.

Perhaps it took political citizenship for granted (which, historically, it has never been safe to do). Civic spirit, citizens' charters and voluntary activity in the community are of crucial importance, but individuals must be helped and prepared to shape the terms of such engagements by political understanding and action. Respect for the rule of law is a necessary condition for any kind of social order and a necessary component of education. In a parliamentary democracy, however, education must also help future citizens distinguish between law and justice. Such a distinction marked the very beginning of political thought in ancient Athens.

Citizens must be equipped with the political skills needed to change laws in a peaceful and responsible manner. We firmly believe that volunteering and community involvement are necessary conditions of civil society and democracy. Preparation for these, at the very least, should be an explicit part of education. This is especially important at a time when government is attempting a shift of emphasis between, on the one hand, state welfare provision and responsibility and, on the other, community and individual responsibility. We say only that while volunteering and voluntary service are necessary conditions for full citizenship in a democracy, they are not sufficient conditions.

Local communities are, indeed, not isolated from the state and public policy. This has recently been well stated by Professor David Hargreaves in a DEMOS pamphlet, The Mosaic of Learning: 'Civic education is about the civic virtues and decent behaviour that adults wish to see in young people. But it is also more than this. Since Aristotle it has been accepted as an inherently political concept that raises questions about the sort of society we live in, how it has come to take its present form, the strengths and weaknesses of current political structures, and how improvements might be made.... Active citizens are as political as they are moral; moral sensibility derives in part from political understanding; political apathy spawns moral apathy.'

So a working definition must be wide, without being all things to everyone, but specifically must identify and relate all three of Marshall's dimensions, not to call any one of them on its own true 'active citizenship'. Active citizenship must be an habitual interaction between all three. While we say that voluntary and community activity cannot be the full meaning of active citizenship, we also recognise that freedom and full citizenship in the political arena itself depends on a society with a rich variety of non-political associations and voluntary groups—what some have called civil society. So what some once argued for, 'political education and political literacy', might now seem too narrow a term to catch our meaning compared to 'citizenship education'.

So what do we mean by 'effective education for citizenship'? We mean three things, related to each other, mutually dependent on each other, but each needing a somewhat different place and treatment in the curriculum: social and moral responsibility, community involvement and political literacy.

Firstly, children learning from the very beginning self-confidence and socially and morally responsible behaviour both in and beyond the classroom, both towards those in authority and towards each other. This learning should be developed, not only in but also beyond school, whenever and wherever children work or play in groups or participate in the affairs of their communities. Some may think this aspect of citizenship hardly needs mentioning; but we believe it to be near the heart of the matter. Here guidance on moral values and personal development are essential preconditions of citizenship.

Some might regard the whole of primary school education as pre-citizenship, certainly pre-political; but this is mistaken. Children are already forming through learning and discussion, concepts of fairness, and attitudes to the law, to rules, to decision-making, to authority, to their local environment and social responsibility etc. They are also picking up, whether from school, home or elsewhere, some knowledge of whether they are living in a democracy or not, of what social problems affect them and even what the different pressure groups or parties have to say about them. All this can be encouraged, guided and built upon.

Secondly, learning about and becoming helpfully involved in the life and concerns of their communities, including learning through community involvement and service to the community. This, of course, like the other two branches of citizenship, is by no means limited to children's time in school. Even if pupils and adults perceive many of the voluntary groups as non-political, the clearer meaning is probably to say 'non-partisan': for voluntary bodies when exercising persuasion, interacting with public authorities, publicising, fund-raising, recruiting members and then trying to activate (or placate) them, all such bodies are plainly using and needing political skills.

Thirdly, pupils learning about and how to make themselves effective in public life through knowledge, skills and values—what can be called 'political literacy', seeking for a term that is wider than political knowledge alone. The term 'public life' is used in its broadest sense to encompass realistic knowledge of and preparation for conflict resolution and decision-making related to the main economic and social problems of the day, including each individual's expectations of and preparations for the world of employment, and discussion of the allocation of public resources and the rationale of taxation. Such preparations are needed whether these problems occur in locally, nationally or internationally concerned organisations or at any level of society from formal political institutions to informal groups, both at local or national level.

So our understanding of citizenship education in a parliamentary democracy finds three heads on one body: social and moral responsibility, community involvement and political literacy. 'Responsibility' is an essential political as well as moral virtue, for it implies

(a) care for others;

(b) premeditation and calculation about what effect actions are likely to have on others; and

(c) understanding and care for the consequences.

Citizenship Education

We state a case for citizenship education being a vital and distinct statutory part of the curriculum, an entitlement for all pupils in its own right. We recognise that citizenship education can be enhanced by and can make significant contributions to—as well as draw upon—other subjects and aspects of the curriculum. We stress, however, that citizenship education is education for citizenship, behaving and acting as a citizen, therefore it is not just knowledge of citizenship and civic society; it also implies developing values, skills and understanding. We also recognise that such an education is linked to two other developments in schools and depends on their effectiveness, especially in the early stages of children's development.

Firstly, the promotion of Personal, Social and Health Education (PSHE); and, secondly, new developments of a kind being piloted by QCA in a whole-school approach to the promotion of pupils' Spiritual, Moral, Social and Cultural development (SMSC). All such work has some social and community entailments.

In September 1997, a Citizenship 2000 group was formed, following initial discussions by representatives of the Citizenship Foundation, the Association for the Teaching of the Social Sciences (ATSS), the Secondary Heads Association (SHA), and the Hansard Society. An agreed statement pointed to 'rapidly changing relationships between the individual and government; the decline in traditional forms of civic cohesion; the new political context of Britain in Europe; and rapid social, economic and technological change in a global context'. So it concluded:

> 'Citizenship education in schools and colleges is too important to be left to chance; recent research has underlined the weakness of civic discourse in this country. Citizenship education is urgently needed to address this historic deficit if we are to avoid a further decline in the quality of our public life and if we are to prepare all young people for informed participation, not only in a more open United Kingdom, but also in Europe and the wider world, as we move into the next century. This will not happen unless there is a firm political and professional commitment to education for citizenship.'

Many reported strong social norms 'never to talk about religion or politics'. Those who had such an opportunity at school, however, were more likely to talk at home or in the community. 'Talk' or discourse is obviously fundamental to active citizenship. When the British sample was asked to give examples of good citizenship only 10 per cent mentioned voting or exercising political rights, whereas 70 per cent 'talked about civic engagement in some form—for example, working in local voluntary associations, doing something beneficial in the local community'. However, the research found that 'single issue' politics figured more largely; 'green' concerns and environmental issues generally attract attention and support.

Perhaps there is some 'displacement effect' at work here: political scientists have suggested for some time that young people, when feeling that 'something ought to be done about it', are less likely than the post-war generation to join political parties, are more likely to join a particular pressure group. Professor Crewe found that more young people stand up for animal rights than for civil or human rights. Even so, here are positive connections between the civil and the political in the minds of young people that we will seek to show could be developed to mutual benefit both by schools and voluntary bodies.

The British Election Study reports that 25 per cent of the 18-24 age group said they would not vote in the 1992 general election, the highest abstention rate among all age groups. In the 1997 general election, the reported figure had risen to 32 per cent abstention, again the highest among all age groups, though MORI put it at 43 per cent. This is compared to 71 per cent actual turn-out in the total electorate (the lowest in the post-war period). There is general acceptance that the actual abstention rate among the 18-24 age group in 1997 will have been greater than that reported.

However, a research study by the Trust for the Study of Adolescence in 1997 found that a majority of its sample had been involved in some form of political or community action the previous year. A MORI survey for the News of the World in March 1997 on first-time voters found that 28 per cent said they would not vote or were unlikely to, 55 per cent said that they were not interested or could not be bothered, 17 per cent said that it would not make any difference, and 10 per cent said they did not trust any politicians. Such are some measures of alienation and cynicism.

Truancy, vandalism, random violence, premeditated crime and habitual drug-taking can be other indicators of youth alienation, even if historical comparisons are difficult; and the spurts, fits and fashions of vivid media coverage can make it difficult to judge how much is real increase and how much is justifiable public intolerance of things once taken more or less for granted. A Social and Community Planning Research (SCPR) survey, commissioned in 1996 by Barnardo's, revealed broadly similar figures. For instance, only 21 per cent of young people claimed to 'support' a political party and 55 per cent said they never read a newspaper.

However, we would comment that such a level of knowledge is so basic that well-taught youngsters in primary school can have it, and often do—and much more—by the age of eight or nine; but others, leaving secondary school, are apparently no better than that. For example, pupils by the age of eleven should know what Parliament stands for and something of how it works and what are its powers.

A DEMOS pamphlet by Helen Wilkinson and Geoff Mulgan, Freedom's Children: work, relationships and politics for 18-34 year olds in Britain today, presented evidence of ignorance and—as it were—'could-not care-less' attitudes, leading them to state a powerful case that there should be a legal obligation to teach civic education alongside personal and social education and for some central responsibility for civic and political education, as in Australia and Canada. (They could also have cited all other countries in the EU.)

Over the whole population, the authors note that disrespect for the way Parliament works doubled in four years after 1991, and that trust in society's core institutions has been falling steadily, leaving only minority support for the way that national government (15 per cent) and local government (25 per cent) works. About a third of young people take pride in being outside and against the mainstream, identifying only with their own sub-cultures. The authors argue that 'the potentially explosive alienation we have uncovered requires a different approach to politics—new style of leadership, new languages and new mechanisms'. Their conclusion has worrying implications for the future of democracy in this country: 'The overwhelming story emerging from our research, both quantitative and qualitative, is of an historic political disconnection. In effect, an entire generation has opted out of party politics.'

Another view, however, is found in a comparison of teenage and adult attitudes to politics based on British Social Attitudes, No 12 (SCPR), 1995-96. Roger Jowell and Alison Park presented these findings in a lecture in December 1997 organised by the Citizenship Foundation, entitled 'Young People, Politics and Citizenship—a disengaged generation?'. They suggested that negative attitudes, ignorance and low voting turn-out among the younger generation (18-24 year olds) were only marginally worse than the next adult cohort, and that the figures improved towards middle age, only dropping off again in old age. So they questioned whether teenage and younger generation alienation was the kind of 'historic political disconnection' of the DEMOS pamphlet, or perhaps a normal phenomenon of the life cycle.

Ignorance was considerable, as was distrust of government and politicians, but the authors pointed out that it was 'not surprising, perhaps' that 12-18 year olds were even less interested and knowledgeable about politics than were 18-24 year-olds; but that as people got older, concerned with taxes, mortgages and family, they began to inform themselves better and show more concern for public policy. Perhaps we need to make only two comments on this complex question: firstly, that the truth could well be somewhere between the historic shift argument and that things are much as ever they were; and secondly that even accepting Jowell and Park's suggestion that things may not be getting dramatically worse, they are inexcusably and damagingly bad, and could and should be remedied.

Schools should have a coherent and sequential programme of citizenship education. There has been a small but important pointer recently to show how values can modify behaviour when mediated through a good teaching programme. The Home Office in 1990 financed a pilot study into teaching about drug abuse, in three inner-London primary schools, called 'Project Charlie'. The results were monitored six years later and a report published in November 1997.

The findings showed a significantly lower level of experimentation with both tobacco and illegal drugs, and greater resistance to peer pressure, in the children who had been taught in the programme compared to schoolmates who had not. There are less tangible but wider social questions that constitute a broader aim for citizenship education. The Citizenship Foundation put the case to the National Commission on Education of 1992 in terms of: 'the increasingly complex nature of our society, the greater cultural diversity and the apparent loss of a value consensus, combined with the collapse of traditional support mechanisms such as extended families...'. 'Cultural diversity' raises the issue of national identity.

Responding to these worries, a main aim for the whole community should be to find or restore a sense of common citizenship, including a national identity that is secure enough to find a place for the plurality of nations, cultures, ethnic identities and religions long found in the United Kingdom. Citizenship education creates common ground between different ethnic and religious identities.

Majorities must respect, understand and tolerate minorities and minorities must learn and respect the laws, codes and conventions as much as the majority—not merely because it is useful to do so, but because this process helps foster common citizenship. This gives a special importance to citizenship education, for these matters of national identity in a pluralist society are complex and should never be taken for granted. We all need to learn more about each other. This should entail learning not only about the United Kingdom—including all four of its component parts—but also about the European, Commonwealth and global dimensions of citizenship, with due regard being given to the homelands of our minority communities and to the main countries of British emigration.

We acknowledge that there may be considerable commonality of values and approach or method, especially in primary schools—but we will differ as to content as pupils progress from primary to secondary school—here these must include explicit knowledge of social and political institutions and processes. Citizenship education is important and distinct enough to warrant a separate specification within the national framework. The British Youth Council (BYC) represents nearly one hundred youth organisations with a nominal membership of some 3 million young people aged between 18 and 25.

The curriculum should enable children and young people to develop an awareness of community and cultural diversity. It should help them see where and how they fit into the community. It should enable them to understand their community, its history, what part it has played in national life etc. It should also enable them to gain an understanding of the diversity of community and society and an awareness of equal opportunities issues, national identity and cultural differences. In addition, the curriculum should show how ordinary citizens have been the catalysts for change and improvement at a local, national and international level.

The curriculum should consider the factors that lead to exclusion from society, such as bullying, colour and other forms of "difference". It should make students aware of the difficulties such exclusion can have on the individual and society and of the reasons why some people "opt out" of the moral social set-up. In looking at these areas, the curriculum should enable children and young people to explore and understand key questions, moral problems and issues that concern society.

The curriculum should also cover practical skills that enable young people to participate effectively in public life and prepare them to be full citizens. It should enable children and young people to develop discussion, communication and teamwork skills. It should help them learn to argue cogently and effectively, negotiate successfully and co-operate with others. It should also enable them to think for themselves, solve problems and make decisions effectively. These practical skills should be backed up by mechanisms that enable children and young people to practise them.

We strongly believe that schools should, where practicable, establish Schools Councils. Schools Councils provide practical first-hand experience of decision-making and democratic processes. They enable children and young people to participate effectively in schools and debate and address issues of concern to them and their school. ' All that is lacking in this statement by the BYC is stress on volunteering and learning from and in the local community, and consideration of economic realities, notably taxation. These it plainly had taken for granted, since most of its constituent organisations are heavily committed to volunteering and community work. A philosopher once said that we often forget to state our major presuppositions.

Plainly the BYC is not saying that the young people it represents did not welcome discussion of the problems it mentions; but it is saying that they feel left up in the air without the teaching of political literacy that could empower them in adult life to have some effect on these problems. To tackle social issues in school problem by problem can be beneficial, when done in some generally acceptable and practical moral framework. Even so, it would not add up to an understanding of politics. For politics is the general process by which differences of values and interests are compromised or mediated through institutions in the general interest.

Learning Outcomes

The learning outcomes are part of a broad framework for citizenship education and learning in schools. This framework provides the basis for what good citizenship education in schools might look like and how it can be successfully delivered. It seeks to build from the aims and purposes of citizenship education, as set out in the initial report, and to bring increasing clarity about what citizenship education entails and how it can be approached, including opportunities within and beyond schools. In this way, the framework seeks to ensure that the benefits to pupils, teachers, schools and society at large of establishing citizenship teaching in schools and community-centred learning and activities are realised.

In particular, the benefits of the framework include: increased clarity for teachers about what they should teach and how they might teach it; specified learning outcomes for pupils; a firmer basis for the assessment of pupils' progress and of the progression in their learning; and a better foundation for schools to coordinate existing teaching approaches and learning opportunities and to relate positively to the local community. Over time, it is hoped that the framework will enhance teachers' confidence and professionalism in developing effective citizenship education for all pupils.

The learning outcomes are founded on a number of guiding principles, and aim to secure:

- *Breadth and balance*: To extend and deepen the range and quality of educational experiences that pupils should have through their schooling;
- *Coherence*: To provide an entitlement to citizenship education which is coherent for pupils in terms of the concepts, values and dispositions, skills and aptitudes and knowledge and understanding to be acquired, and the range of educational experiences;
- *Continuity and progression*: To ensure continuity and progression in pupils' learning through outcomes which are developmental and sequential, and which reinforce and further develop the concepts, values and dispositions, skills and aptitudes and knowledge and understanding which pupils acquire at each key stage;
- *Relevance*: To address the immediate and future needs and interests of pupils in the context of the social,

moral, cultural, political and economic environment; and to contribute to pupils' development of positive attitudes to teaching, the school and society in general;

- *Quality*: To challenge teachers and help pupils to achieve the highest possible standards of excellence, with due regard to differing aptitudes, abilities and circumstances;
- *Access and inclusion*: To ensure that all pupils should have opportunities to engage in all the teaching, activities and experiences which constitute effective education for citizenship.

It is important to recognise that these guiding principles are not exclusive to citizenship education but are part of the general aims and priorities of the curriculum in schools. Learning in citizenship education is influenced by a `umber of factors:

Whole-school approaches: There is increasing recognition that the ethos, organisation, structures and daily practices of schools, including whole-school activities and assemblies have a significant impact on the effectiveness of citizenship education. Through such climate and practices schools provide implicit and explicit messages which can have a considerable influence, both positive and negative, on pupils' learning and development. Schools need to consider how far their ethos, organisation and daily practices are consistent with the aim and purpose of citizenship education and affirm and extend the development of pupils into active citizens.

In particular, schools should make every effort to engage pupils in discussion and consultation about all aspects of school life on which pupils might reasonably be expected to have a view, and wherever possible to give pupils responsibility and experience in helping to run parts of the school. This might include school facilities, organisation, rules, relationships and matters relating to teaching and learning. Such engagement can be through both formal structures such as school and class councils and informal channels in pupils' daily encounters with aspects of school life. To create a feeling that it is 'our school' can increase pupil motivation to learn in all subjects.

Teaching approaches and learning opportunities: The learning outcomes will be best achieved through a broad range of teaching approaches and learning opportunities. These should be chosen for their appropriateness in supporting and challenging pupils in their development, application and understanding of the essential elements underpinning citizenship education and in the overall development of pupils into informed and active citizens. It is vital that pupils are provided with structured opportunities to explore actively aspects, issues and events through school and community involvement, case studies and critical discussions that are challenging and relevant to their lives. It is difficult to conceive of pupils as active citizens if their experience of learning in citizenship education has been predominantly passive.

Pupils may derive further benefit where these opportunities are linked to a class, school or community project which they have helped to identify, plan, carry through and evaluate. Often the school and its local community provide a perfect context for pupils to examine issues and events and to become involved in active, participatory activities and experiences where the emphasis is on learning through action. This can help pupils to make the connection between learning and acting locally to thinking globally.

Special educational needs: There is a need to provide pupils identified with special educational needs with appropriately challenging work in citizenship education at each key stage. This should be in line with the statement on access, which applies to the revised National Curriculum, in the section on Common Requirements. This currently says that: 'The programme of study for each key stage should be taught to the great majority of pupils in the key stage, in ways appropriate to their abilities. For the small number of pupils who may need the provision, material may be selected from earlier or later key stages where this is necessary to enable individual pupils to progress and demonstrate achievement.

Appropriate provision should be made for pupils who need to use:

- means of communication other than speech, including computers, technological aids, signing, symbols or lip-reading;
- non-sighted methods of reading, such as Braille, or non-visual or non-aural ways of acquiring information;
- technological aids in practical and written work;
- aids or adapted equipment to allow access to practical activities within and beyond school.'

Teaching and Learning in Citizenship Education

Day-to-day assessment supports teaching and learning in citizenship education. It helps teachers to clarify their learning objectives and articulate them to pupils, and provides a measure of the progress that pupils have made in the learning outcomes. Such assessment should be practicable and manageable, providing useful information to the parties involved without becoming burdensome.

Day-to-day assessment will take a number of forms, including observation, listening and appraising pupils' written work. This assessment is most effective where it arises naturally from the teaching approaches, learning opportunities and experiences. It should be valued by pupils and raise their standards of achievement in citizenship.

Day-to-day assessment will contribute to periodic reporting on standards and progress and ultimately to pupils' Records of Achievement. At Key Stage 4, it is important that there are opportunities for pupils to receive accreditation for their work in citizenship. Awarding bodies should be encouraged to develop a range of appropriate qualifications to match the needs of young adolescents, including full, combined and short course GCSEs, GNVQ units, and Certificates of Achievement. The framework of learning outcomes has four interrelated components. A clear understanding of the four components and the ways they relate to each other will help teachers use the framework to develop a variety of teaching approaches, learning opportunities and experiences which, together, constitute effective education for citizenship in schools.

Aim and purpose

The purpose of citizenship education in schools and colleges is to make secure and to increase the knowledge, skills and values relevant to the nature and practices of participative democracy; also to enhance the awareness of rights and duties, and the sense of responsibilities needed for the development of pupils into active citizens; and in so doing to establish the value to individuals, schools and society of involvement in the local and wider community.

Democratic institutions, practices and purposes must be understood, both local and national, including the work of parliaments, councils, parties, pressure groups and voluntary bodies; to show how formal political activity relates to civil society in the context of the United Kingdom and Europe, and to cultivate awareness and concern for world affairs and global issues. Some understanding of the realities of economic life is needed including how taxation and public expenditure work together.

Strands

- *Social and Moral Responsibility*: Children learning from the very beginning self-confidence and socially and morally responsible behaviour both in and beyond the classroom, both towards those in authority and towards each other (this is an essential pre-condition for citizenship).
- *Community involvement*: Pupils learning about and becoming helpfully involved in the life and concerns of their communities, including learning through community involvement and service to the community.
- *Political literacy*: Pupils learning about and how to make themselves effective in public life through knowledge, skills and values.

Essential elements

The learning outcomes that follow are founded on four essential elements: concepts; values and dispositions; skills and aptitudes and knowledge and understanding which underpin education for citizenship. The successful integration and progressive development of these essential elements across the key stages should ensure that schools achieve the learning outcomes and in so doing develop effective education for citizenship for all pupils.

Concepts: A number of key concepts provide a clear, overarching, conceptual core to citizenship education. Pupils should come to understand, as they progress through the key stages, how these key concepts serve collectively, though not exclusively, to underpin effective education for citizenship.

Values and dispositions: Certain values and dispositions are appropriate to citizenship education. Pupils should be encouraged, as they progress through the key stages, to recognise, reflect and act upon these values and dispositions. They should be helped, in particular, to reflect on and recognise values and dispositions which underlie their attitudes and actions as individuals and as members of groups or communities. This is vital in developing pupils into active citizens who have positive attitudes to themselves, as individuals, and in their relationship with others.

Skills and aptitudes: Certain skills and aptitudes are appropriate to citizenship education. Pupils should have opportunities to develop and apply these skills and aptitudes within pluralist contexts. These contexts should be carefully chosen in order to allow pupils to reinforce and further deepen their understanding, think critically, develop their own ideas, respond in different ways to a diversity of views, defend or change an opinion, and recognise the contribution of others.

Knowledge and understanding: Pupils should acquire basic knowledge and understanding of particular aspects of society with which citizenship education is concerned.

It must be stressed that the manner and depth of acquisition is a matter for the professional judgement of teachers, taking into account what is appropriate for the age and abilities of the pupils concerned. These particular aspects of society provide important contexts and content to support the aim and purpose of citizenship education in schools and are:

– social;

– moral;

– political, including issues relating to government, law and constitution;

– economic (public and personal), including issues relating to public services, taxation, public expenditure and employment;

– environmental and sustainable development.

Pupils should acquire a basic knowledge and understanding of these aspects of society through the topical and contemporary issues, events and activities which are the lifeblood of citizenship education. The importance should be stressed of developing the habit of having a view on current affairs. The critical reading of newspapers and discussion of television and radio current affairs programmes should be encouraged. For each of these aspects there might be a school, local, national, Europe, Commonwealth or global context.

Some issues and events will allow several of these aspects to be accessed at the same time—others may be more homogeneous. How aspects and topical and contemporary issues and events are selected and treated is a matter for the professional judgement of teachers, taking into account factors such as the age of pupils, the range of their abilities and the relevance and challenge to pupil needs and interests. However, motivation is obviously increased when pupils are given some choice in the issues to be discussed. It should be emphasised that the knowledge and understanding components should not be learned as a disembodied list of aspects, content and terms but embedded in issues, events and activities of significance and interest.

Indeed there is scope, where aspects, content and terms are revisited across key stages, to reinforce and deepen pupils' knowledge and understanding, ensuring continuity and progression in learning. Such an approach is vital in order to achieve the overall aim and purpose of citizenship education in schools. The concepts, and values and dispositions, and, to a much lesser extent, skills and aptitudes, and knowledge and understanding which underpin the learning outcomes are neither inclusive to citizenship education nor mutually exclusive. They can be developed and applied within other subjects and parts of the curriculum.

It will be important for schools to identify the links between pupils' learning, activities and experiences in citizenship education and those elsewhere in the curriculum, both within and beyond the school. This is essential if teachers are to be helped to build on such links in order to reinforce and further develop such learning for pupils and ensure breadth and balance, coherence, continuity and progression and quality in such learning experiences across the curriculum.

Learning outcomes

The learning outcomes are designed so that pupils will be encouraged to develop and apply the skills and aptitudes through the contexts and content provided in the knowledge and understanding components at each key stage. The knowledge and understanding required will be at a basic level. It is important to reiterate that the manner of acquisition is a matter for the professional judgement of teachers taking into account, what is appropriate to the age and abilities of the pupils concerned. In this way, pupils' learning in citizenship education is manageable and capable of being reinforced and further developed as they progress through the key stages.

Key Stage 1

1. *Skills and Aptitudes*: By the end of Key Stage 1, pupils should be able to:
   - express and justify orally a personal opinion relevant to an issue;
   - contribute to paired and class discussion on matters of personal and general significance, learning what it means to take turns, respond to the views of others and use acceptable forms of disagreement or challenge;
   - work with others and gather their opinions in an attempt to meet a challenge of shared significance;
   - use imagination when considering the experience of others;
   - reflect on issues of social and moral concern, presented in different ways such as through story, drama, pictures, poetry, and 'real life' incidents;
   - take part in a simple debate and vote on an issue.
2. *Knowledge and Understanding*: By the end of Key Stage 1, pupils should:

- recognise how the concept of fairness can be applied in a reasoned and reflective way to aspects of their personal and social life;
- understand the different kinds of responsibility that they take on, in helping others, respecting differences or looking after shared property;
- know about the nature and basis of the rules in the classroom, at school and at home; also, whenever possible, know how to frame rules themselves; understand that different rules can apply in different contexts and can serve different purposes, including safety, safeguarding of property and the prevention of unacceptable behaviour;
- know about the different kinds of relationships which exist between pupils and between adults and pupils; also have some notion that the power in such relationships can be exercised responsibly and fairly or irresponsibly and unfairly;
- understand the language used to describe feelings associated with aspects of relationships with others, including words such as happy, sad, disappointed, angry, upset, shy, embarrassed, peaceful, worried, proud and glad;
- understand different kinds of behaviour using moral categories such as kind or unkind, good or bad, right or wrong; know about the consequences of anti-social or egocentric behaviour and attitudes, for individuals and communities; also understand that many problems can be tackled as a community;
- know where they live, in relation to their local and national community, understand that there are different types and groups of people living in their

local community such as other children, teenagers, families and old people;

- know about differences and similarities between people in terms of their needs, rights, responsibilities, wants, likes, values and beliefs; also understand that many of these differences are linked with cultural and religious diversity;
- know and understand, through shared activities and the process of exploratory talk, the meaning of key terms such as respect or disrespect, question, comment, discuss, agree or disagree, similar or different, point of view, opinion, compare and contrast

Key Stage 2

1. *Skills and Aptitudes*: By the end of Key Stage 2, pupils should be able to:
   - express and justify, orally and/or in writing, a personal opinion relevant to an issue;
   - contribute to paired and small group discussion on matters of personal and general significance and be prepared to present the outcome to a class;
   - work with others in a class and gather their opinions in an attempt to meet a challenge of shared significance through negotiation, accommodation and agreed action;
   - use imagination when considering the experience of others and be able to reflect and hypothesise—the 'what if' scenario—on issues of social, moral and political concern in response to stories, drama or 'real life' incidents. These should cover a range of citizenship issues and include consideration of the

lives of others living in other places or times and with different values or customs;

- discuss a range of moral dilemmas or problems, in which choices between alternatives are evaluated, selected and justified, using appropriate language;
- participate in a question and answer session in which a member of the local community offers an expert opinion and answers questions prepared in advance by pupils;
- collect information about a topical or contemporary issue from a range of sources, including television and radio news, documentary footage, newspapers and new communications technologies, and recognise the different ways the sources present the information;
- take part in simple debates and have opportunities to vote on issues.

2. *Knowledge and Understanding*: By the end of Key Stage 2, pupils should:

- know at a simple level, how rules and laws are made and the varying purposes they serve; and understand that there are various sources of authority in their duties but that there are also sources of help and support when needed; also understand the meaning of terms such as rights and responsibilities, right, wrong, fair, unfair, rule, law, forgiveness;
- understand the need for laws and their enforcement in shaping behaviour and tackling crimes and why certain behaviour is prohibited; also know about the role of the police in the prevention of crime and

protection of persons and property, and be aware of the consequences of anti-social behaviour on individuals and communities; also understand the meaning of terms such as punishment, cause, consequence, justice, fairness, evidence;

- know about the workings of local and national communities, including the main faiths and ethnic cultures, and how individuals relate to them; know about, in simple terms, contemporary relations between England, Scotland, Wales and Northern Ireland and Europe; know about local and national sources of government and opportunities to participate; also understand the meaning of terms such as mayor, council, councillor, Member of Parliament (MP), election, vote, parliament, Member of the European Parliament (MEP), political party;
- understand that there can be different types of government such as democracies and dictatorships, also understand the meaning of terms such as freedom of speech, opposition, vote, government, King, Queen, Prime Minister, President;
- know about voluntary and community bodies who work in their local community; also understand the meaning of terms such as voluntary service, volunteer, charity, protest, petition;
- know that there are different economic systems; know that there are different ways of allocating scarce resources; understand the choices that have to be made in modern society and the impact on individuals and communities; also understand the meaning of terms such as fairness, justice, choice, price, services, wealth, market, wage;

- know about the world as a global community, and that people around the world live in communities as we do; understand that there are similarities and differences between communities in terms of social, economic, cultural, political and environmental circumstances; also understand the meaning of terms such as poverty, famine, disease, charity, aid, human rights.

Key Stage 3

1. *Skills and Aptitudes*: By the end of Key Stage 3, pupils should be able to:

   - express and justify, orally and in writing, a personal opinion relevant to an issue;
   - to small group and class discussions on matters of personal and general significance and present the outcome to a class;
   - work with others to meet a challenge of shared significance through negotiation, accommodation and agreed action, and be able to reflect on the process;
   - use imagination when considering the experience of others and be able to role-play, express plausibly and reflect on viewpoints contrary to their own;
   - analyse, discuss and reflect on significant issues and events encountered within a community;
   - garner information about an issue from a range of sources including TV and radio news, documentary footage, newspapers and new communications technologies with some understanding of the different roles these sources play;

- demonstrate an understanding of the use of statistics;
- take part in informal debates and have opportunities to vote on issues.

2. *Knowledge and Understanding*: By the end of Key Stage 3, pupils should:

- understand the significant aspects of topical and contemporary issues and events;
- understand, at a basic level, the legal rights and responsibilities of young people with particular reference to the UN Convention on the Rights of the Child, particularly the right to be heard; understand the general nature of legal aspects and responsibilities of other citizens, including consumer law, employment law, discrimination law, age-related laws and the laws relating to drugs and relationships; also understand the meaning of terms such as discrimination, equal opportunities, tribunal, ballot, trade unions;
- understand the rights and responsibilities underpinning a democratic society, with particular reference to the European Convention on Human Rights (ECHR); be aware of issues surrounding rights such as freedom of speech and freedom from arbitrary arrest; know about the Universal Declaration of Human Rights and why it was developed; also understand the meaning of terms such as prejudice, xenophobia, discrimination, pluralism;
- know about aspects of the criminal justice system, including the role of the police and how a criminal trial works; also understand the meaning of terms

such as court, judge, magistrate, jury, witness, defendant;

- know about local government, the services it offers and the opportunities to contribute at a local level; also understand the meaning of terms such as mayor, council, councillor, bye-law, election;
- know about the work of voluntary and community bodies; also understand the meaning of terms such as pressure groups, lobbying, protest, public opinion;
- know about the work of Parliament, the Government and the Executive in making and changing the law; also understand the meaning of terms such as Member of Parliament (MP), general election, political party, national government, opposition, cabinet, government department, Act of parliament;
- know about the ideas and aims of the main political parties and pressure groups; also understand the meaning of terms such as pressure groups, lobbying, public opinion;
- know about the UK as a political entity, including its multi-national constitution and contemporary relations with the Republic of Ireland, the European Union (EU) and the Commonwealth; also understand the meaning of terms such as Scottish Parliament, Northern Ireland Assembly, Welsh Assembly, Member of the European Parliament (MEP), European Union (EU);
- understand the economic system with reference to the work of the marketand the concept of price and major economic issues of the day such as poverty

and unemployment, including the provision of key public services; also understand the meaning of terms such as taxation, the welfare state, competition, market forces, distribution of wealth;

– know about the world as a global community and understand the political, economic and social disparities that exist; also understand the meaning of terms such as overseas aid, development, sustainable development, international trade, charity, human rights.

Key Stage 4

1. *Skills and Aptitudes*: By the end of Key Stage 4, pupils should be able to:

   – express and justify, orally and in writing, a personal opinion relevant to an issue;

   – contribute to small group and class discussions on matters of personal and general significance and present the outcome to a wider audience;

   – work with others to meet a challenge of shared significance through negotiation, accommodation and agreed action, and be able to reflect on and critically evaluate the process;

   – use imagination when considering the experience of others and be able to role-play and express plausibly viewpoints contrary to their own, and to reflect on and critically evaluate such viewpoints;

   – investigate, analyse, discuss and reflect on major challenges faced by communities;

   – research an issue or event of significance from a range of sources including TV and radio news, documentary footage, newspapers and new communications technologies with particular reference to bias and the use of evidence;

- demonstrate an understanding of the use and abuse of statistics;
- take part in formal debates and have structured opportunities to vote on issues.

2. *Knowledge and Understanding*: By the end of Key Stage 4 pupils should:

   - understand the significant aspects of topical and contemporary issues and events;
   - understand, at a basic level, the law and the legal system in relation to areas such as the family, consumers, the law at work and in relation to the environment; understand about different sources and types of law, including statute, judge-made law, and European law (including ECHR); know about the different ways in which the law is enforced, the role of the police, crime and punishment and penal reform as a personal and social issue; also understand the meaning of terms such as rule of law, civil law, criminal law, civil rights, natural justice;
   - know about the different ways in which MPs can be elected and the Government held accountable through parliament to the electorate, including the importance of voting, public opinion, opinion polls, the role of the media, lobbying, pressure groups and different forms of protest; the different electoral systems and understand the reasons for the differences; also understand the meaning of terms such as proportional representation, referendum, federalism, monarchy;

- know about the values, interests and policies of the main political parties and pressure groups; also understand the meaning of terms such as pressure groups, lobbying, public opinion;
- know about the changing constitution of the UK, including the relationship between the two Houses of Parliament, the changing role of the monarchy, shifting relationships between England, Scotland, Wales and Northern Ireland and Britain's relationship with the European Union and the Commonwealth; some understanding of why the European Union was created; also understand the meaning of terms such as devolution, independence, European Monetary Union (EMU);
- understand the economic system with reference to what is appropriate to private and to public ownership, regulation or control, and to problems of income distribution, employment, taxation, housing and the provision of public services, especially health, education and social services; also understand the meaning of terms such as wealth creation, personal taxation, pension provision;
- understand the world as a global community, including issues such as sustainable development, economic interdependence, heavily indebted countries, and the work of United Nations organisations and majornon-governmental organisations; understand the meaning of terms such as stewardship, interdependence, ethical trading, peace-making and peacekeeping.

The word 'elements' is important for we strongly believe that citizenship needs a distinct profile in the revised curriculum. Though some of the key concepts, values and dispositions, and skills and aptitudes in the learning outcomes can be developed and applied within other parts of the curriculum, many of the skills and aptitudes, and knowledge and understanding need separate articulation. Nonetheless in primary schools this is likely to be done by class teachers through existing subjects and there can be substantial overlap.

The biggest overlap is with PSE or PSHE. In History, there is much teaching and learning about the development of societies and of political, social and economic systems, including the development of British democracy and of our pluralist society, which provides an essential conceptual and institutional foundation to many elements in our learning outcomes. For example, the history of Parliament is at the heart of British history and can readily lead into discussion of present day electoral arrangements.

Meanwhile, British, European and world history topics can also lead into consideration of the international, sustainable development and the human rights aspects of our learning outcomes. The emphasis in History on the use of evidence and processes of enquiry can help pupils to discuss and reach informed judgements about topical and contemporary issues which are the lifeblood of citizenship and to develop the confidence to take informed action.

In Geography, the emphasis of place, space and environment and the study of places, themes and issues from the local to the global, offers significant opportunities to learn about conflicts and concerns, to extend knowledge about political groupings and the activities of pressure groups and voluntary bodies and to evaluate the consequences for people, places and environments of decision-making. There is a particular opportunity to understand how people and places are inextricably linked and interdependent, thus to learn about and experience citizenship from the local to the global.

The processes of enquiry in Geography, as in History, can also contribute to pupils' development of the understanding, skills and confidence needed to take informed action. Pupil involvement in fieldwork can enhance such learning and despite the pressure of the timetable, many schools in Key Stage 3 have Environmental Studies programmes. While in most secondary schools with existing citizenship programmes of some kind the teaching is done by History and Geography teachers, English can also play a role.

There is scope through the sources in English teaching to make links to the elements in our learning outcomes—both printed sources (books, plays, poems and newspapers) and oral and visual sources (television, radio, and new communications technologies)—as well as through drama, role-play, literary criticism and media education. One common example is reading Orwell's Animal Farm. Is it a lament for the failed attempt to create an egalitarian society, or an implication that it was and is always impossible?

The critical, open-ended reading and discussion of a text is a skill very close to our 'critical approach to evidence put before one and ability to look for fresh evidence'. Meanwhile, drama, role-play and stories can be excellent means to help pupils develop the 'ability to consider and appreciate the experience of others'. The possibility of combination is not limited to History, Geography and English, though these are likely to be closest to citizenship in terms of subject content, contexts and teaching and learning approaches.

Other subjects can make valuable contributions too. For example Mathematics and Information Technology (IT) can contribute to a knowledge and understanding of electoral systems and opinion polls and the skills to get the best from them. Science and Technology subjects commonly raise ethical issues of social policy. Religious Education (RE) provides opportunities to explore moral and social concerns.

Physical Education (PE) can encourage individual initiative and effort as well as teamwork skills. Modern Foreign Languages (MFL) can offer a contrasting perspective from other countries on national, European and international events and issues, while Business Studies can combine to exemplify the economic aspects of citizenship. The experience of the Technical and Vocational Education Initiative (TVEI) highlighted the existing possibilities in making combinations with music and the arts. One obvious linkage of Art, citizenship, PSE and PSHE exists already in many schools where classroom walls and open areas are covered with artwork made by pupils, illustrative of lessons and projects. These are but a few illustrative examples to underline the possibilities.

The potential combinations are many and varied. How these combinations are identified and approached is ultimately a matter for schools to decide, so long as they are natural and advantageous to the subjects involved and the elements of citizenship education in any combinations are clearly identifiable. Many schools are able to find time for programmes based on the ideas of Human Rights, Rights of the Child, Global Citizenship or Sustainable Development, and the charters or international agreements associated with them.

Others find room simply for a weekly current affairs lesson. All of these can make and are making (where they occur) significant contributions to citizenship learning and teaching. In our general aims and learning outcomes they can all find a valued place; but none on their own can furnish the comprehensive and sequential citizenship teaching of our advice. Nonetheless, our strategy allows for considerable variation in the proportion of time and effort given to different topics and existing programmes.

We recognise the close links between citizenship and 'the six key skills' (communication, application of number, information technology, working with others, improving own learning and performance, and problem solving and learning) and maintain that citizenship learning can be a relevant and an appropriate context for pupils' development and achievement of key skills. Our proposed learning outcomes provide many opportunities to integrate the key skills; an approach that would avoid duplication of effort and be of greater benefit to pupils and schools. The first three key skills are at the heart of the learning outcomes across all four key stages.

The key skill of Communication closely relates to the emphasis in citizenship on discussion and the opportunities for pupils to develop and practise verbal communication skills from primary school onward. This should be seen alongside the current emphasis on literacy which overlaps with the skill in citizenship of gathering and critically evaluating information and evidence in all forms. There are numerous opportunities through citizenship learning to help pupils to progress in their written and verbal communication skills and the ability to develop a reasoned argument. The key skill of Application of Number can also be developed in citizenship contexts, such as examining electoral systems, opinion polls and statistics and investigating the current reforms to the electoral system in Britain.

The teaching of citizenship can contribute to the key skill of Information Technology (IT) by enabling pupils to develop their competence in, for example, data handling and presentation of information. Good use can be made of Information and Communications Technology (ICT) in teaching citizenship education where it enables the learning outcomes to be achieved more effectively. The teaching and learning of some topics can be enhanced through the use of software packages and websites. The wider key skills, though closely interrelated, can also be developed through the teaching approaches and learning opportunities which underpin the learning outcomes in citizenship.

The key skill of Working with Others is fundamental to the aim and purpose of citizenship education and to help pupils become involved in the local and wider community. The key skill of Improving Own Learning and Performance is a guiding principle behind the learning outcomes, while the key skill of Problem Solving can be developed through an active, experimental approach to citizenship both inside and outside schools. We see problem-solving as central to political and social thinking in education, rather than formulation of doctrinal alternatives—as some have argued.

We also note the potential of the day to day approaches to assessment of learning in citizenship education in schools to contribute to the assessment of pupils' development and acquisition of key skills. The recording of citizenship learning through pupil Records of Achievement and other appropriate forms of accreditation, offer scope to the future development of key skills qualifications both pre and post-sixteen.

Whole-School Issues

We recognise the significant contribution that citizenship learning can make to whole-school issues and to the development of values. The contribution is a two-way process. The ethos, organisation, structures and daily practices of schools have a considerable impact on the effectiveness of citizenship education. Schools need to consider to what extent their ethos, organisation and daily practices are consistent with the aim and purpose of citizenship education, and provide opportunities for pupils to develop into active citizens.

We believe that schools should make every effort to engage pupils in discussion and consultation about all aspects of school life on which pupils might reasonably be expected to have a view, and wherever possible to give pupils responsibility and experience in helping to run parts of the school. Citizenship learning can also make a significant contribution to the development of values. The values and dispositions which underpin citizenship and democratic politics are clearly set out in the learning outcomes.

Pupils are encouraged to recognise, reflect and act upon these values and dispositions through citizenship learning across the four key stages. These values and dispositions overlap with, though are not restricted by, the values in the context of society, identified in PSHE and by the National Forum for Values in Education and in the community, which form the basis of the QCA pilot looking at a whole-school approach to the promotion of pupils' Spiritual, Moral, Social and Cultural development.

3

Elements of Education for Democracy

The rising tide of international interest in education for democracy has stimulated fresh thinking about education for democracy. Ten essential elements of a good education for democracy are necessary, if not sufficient, to the preparation of students for civic and political life in any country undergoing transition to democracy. And these ten essential elements are necessary to the maintenance of democracy in any country that has it and wants to keep it. These elements certainly are not all there is to a good education for democracy; as you know, there is more to it.

But, without these elements, education for democracy is not complete, and it is not likely to achieve its goals. The maintenance and improvement of democracy in the United State of America or anywhere else will not happen unless there is good education for democracy in schools, which transmits to each new generation of children the basic knowledge, skills, and dispositions by which citizens make their democracy work.

So, if we would maintain and improve democracy by teaching it effectively, then we must emphasise the essential elements of education for democracy in the curriculum of schools, in the teaching and learning of students, and in the university-based preparation of teachers. The task of making a transition to democracy and then sustaining it can be difficult, as the recent history of post-communist countries has shown us. Each of these ten elements are briefly described below.

The first essential element of a good education for democracy is a systematic and continual emphasis on teaching and learning knowledge of democracy, democratic government, and democratic society. If students would be prepared for effective and responsible participation in a democracy, then they must know what it is and what is it not. They must know the standards or criteria by which we distinguish democratic governments and societies from those that are not democratic.

Most scholars agree about the minimal standard by which to judge whether or not a government is a democracy: it is minimally a democracy if the people's representatives in government are elected in free, fair, open, and competitive elections; and the electorate is inclusive so that a large majority of the people who live under the government's authority have the right to vote. Thus, there is government by consent of the governed in which the people's representatives are accountable to the people.

If our students are to be well educated about the concept of democracy, however, they need to know more than the minimal definition that pertains only to standards for conducting elections of the people's representatives in government. They must learn that a more fully developed democracy exceeds the minimal electoral standard by providing constitutional guarantees for civil liberties and human rights of all the people living in the society under the government's authority. In a fully developed democracy, there is a people's government, which is limited by the supreme law of the people's Constitution, for the purpose of protecting equally, through the rule of law, the rights of everyone in the society.

In particular, there is constitutional protection for the individual's rights to think, speak, decide, and act freely to influence the policies and actions of the government. Thus, there is majority rule with protection of the human rights of everyone, including individuals in the minority. The most rigorous test of whether or not a society is fully democratic and free, with human rights and justice for all, is in two questions: Are the society's most unpopular individuals and groups secure in their enjoyment of human rights? And do they enjoy justice under the law on equal terms with others in the society? If the answer is yes, then the government and society are perfectly democratic and free.

However, not even one government and society in the world perfectly meets this test. There is no such thing as a perfect democracy, and there never will be. Rather, the best democratic governments and societies are the least imperfect ones-the ones that come closest to the standards by which we distinguish democracies from non-democracies and compare and evaluate various democratic governments. At present, according to the annual global surveys of Freedom House, an American nongovernmental organisation, less than half of the world's democracies sufficiently satisfy the most stringent criteria by which they may achieve the highest rating for democracy and freedom, because they really attempt to protect the human rights of all citizens. If students would have a good education for democracy, they should learn how to use the criteria by which we minimally distinguish a democracy from a nondemocracy and a more fully developed and free democracy from one that is less developed and less free.

The second essential element of a good education for democracy is teaching and learning knowledge of the Constitution and institutions of the democratic government and civil society in which the students live. A good education for democracy in any country necessarily includes systematic instruction about the principles of the Constitution, the institutions of government under this Constitution, and the nongovernmental institutions that constitute the civil society. As they learn about the constitutional government and civil society of their country, students should be challenged continuously to use the criteria by which we recognise a democracy to assess or critically appraise the extent to which their own governmental institutions and civil society organisations are or are not in conformity with worldwide standards for democracy and human rights.

And students should be asked to compare their government and civil society with the governments and civil societies of other nations in terms of the generally accepted criteria for democracy. They should be challenged to make judgments about whether or not their government and civil society are more or less democratic and free than those of other countries.

The third essential element in a good education for democracy is development of the student's propensity and capacity to apply or use knowledge to think and participate competently in a democracy. Basic knowledge of democracy-its principles, practices, and history-ought to be applied by individuals to the civic and political events of the past and present; if so, this knowledge can be learned thoroughly and used constructively in their lives. So, students need to learn skills of cognition and skills of participation in concert with their acquisition of knowledge.

Cognitive skills enable individuals to identify, describe, organise, interpret, explain, and evaluate information and ideas in order to make sense of their experiences and to make decisions about them. If students develop cognitive skills, they can respond to their experiences reasonably and effectively, and when confronted by a public issue, for example, they can make and defend decisions about the matter, as a good citizen should do. Participation skills, used in concert with cognitive skills, enable individuals to cooperate with others to monitor and influence the actions and decisions of their government and to make their representatives in government accountable to them.

Participation skills, when conjoined with cognitive skills, also enable individuals to cooperate with others as leaders and followers in the nongovernmental organisations that constitute their civil society and thereby to act for the common good. So, education for democracy in schools must include lessons and projects that involve students cooperatively in active learning of skills that enable them to participate constructively in their government and civil society.

The fourth essential element of a good education for democracy involves the development of civic virtue and the behavioral dispositions of the good citizen in a democracy. Civic virtue entails the subordination of personal interests to the common good of the community to which one belongs. If students would develop civic virtue, they must practice the behavioral dispositions or habits of the good citizen in a democracy. Examples of these democratic dispositions are temperance or self-control, fortitude or courage, commitment to justice or fairness, prudence, charity or compassion for others, hope or optimism about the future, honesty or fidelity to the truth, civility in dealings with others, tolerance, and respect for the equal worth and dignity of each person in recognition of the equal humanity of each one. These traits of good character constitute the morality of democratic citizenship.

Alexis de Tocqueville, the Frenchman who went to the United States in the 1830s and wrote Democracy in America, was impressed by the democratic dispositions of Americans, who readily gave their time, money, and other resources to the nongovernmental associations of their civil society, which contributed extensively to the common good. He called these behavioral dispositions "the habits of the heart" and claimed that democracy could not work without them. According to Tocqueville, a country with the very best constitution, institutions, and laws will not have a sustainable democracy unless "the habits of the heart" are firmly implanted in the character of the citizens. So, students in schools must be involved in activities that require them to demonstrate civic virtue through persistent practice of the dispositions or traits of morality that sustain a healthy and vibrant democracy.

The fifth essential element of a good education for democracy is the systematic connection and integration of basic knowledge, skills, and dispositions in the curriculum and instruction presented to students. Effective teaching of knowledge about democracy requires that it be integrated with skills of cognition, skills of participation, and moral dispositions of the good citizen. All the necessary components of a good education for democracy-knowledge, skills, and dispositions-must be continually connected through activities that involve application of knowledge through the persistent practice of skills and dispositions.

Elevation of one component of education for democracy over the other components-for example, knowledge over skills and dispositions or viceversa—is a flaw that impedes teaching and learning about the theory and practice of democracy. So, basic knowledge, skills, and dispositions must be combined and connected continually, systematically, and dynamically to bring about an effective education for democracy. Core content, however, is the indispensable foundation of an effective education for democracy. Individuals who have a deep and abiding comprehension of the prevailing principles of democracy-the big ideas that define democratic government and citizenship-are more likely than others to exhibit several desirable virtues or dispositions of democratic citizenship, such as a propensity to vote and otherwise participate in political and civic life, a sense of political tolerance, a sense of political efficacy, political interest, and concern for the common good of the community.

Furthermore, students who comprehend key concepts in the theory and practice of democracy tend to be adept in their use of such cognitive skills as organisation and interpretation of information; and they are more likely than others to know and retain information about political institutions and events. Examples of the concepts that should be at the core of a good education for democracy are representative government, popular sovereignty, constitutionalism or the rule of law, human rights, responsible citizenship, civil society, and market economy.

The sixth essential element of a good education for democracy is to teach knowledge, skills, and dispositions of democracy throughout the curriculum of the school. Teaching and learning the knowledge, skills, and dispositions of democracy should begin in the primary school and continue at every grade or level to the completion of secondary school or high school. And there should be lessons about democracy in various school subjects, such as history, literature, economics, and geography in addition to separate courses in the subjects of civics and government. As students move from lower to higher grades in schools, they should study more complexly and deeply the same ideas, skills, and dispositions that constitute the core of a good education for democracy. Thus, they might master these ideas, skills, and dispositions by the time they complete their last required year of school.

The seventh essential element of a good education for democracy is involvement of students in extracurricular activities that can be connected to the formal teaching and learning experiences required by the curriculum and conducted by teachers in the classrooms of schools. There is a strong relationship between participation in student organisations and team sports and achievement of democratic skills and dispositions. In particular, participation in student government activities can provide opportunities for learning democracy by doing it.

Desirable outcomes are maximised, however, when there are strong connections between learning experiences within the curriculum and those in extracurricular activities. Development of students' democratic skills and dispositions through extracurricular activities is enhanced when an ethos or spirit of democracy pervades the meetings of student organisations as a consequence of the school's administrative policies.

The eighth essential element of a good education for democracy is the teacher-led discussion of current events and issues in an open classroom in which the environment is conducive to and supportive of a free exchange of information and ideas, and where there is mutual tolerance for diverse opinions. Students' achievement of democratic skills and dispositions is increased greatly when the teacher establishes and maintains a democratic ethos in the classroom, which encourages free and open expression of ideas, security for freedom of inquiry, and respect for the dignity and worth of each person in the group.

However, when leading class discussions of current events or public issues, the teacher should remember the primary importance of content or subject matter anchored in core concepts, because this is the foundation of a sound education for democracy. Superficial discussions of trendy topics or current events, which are separated from basic knowledge of the subject, are not likely to yield significant and enduring gains in the student's competence for citizenship in a democracy.

The ninth essential element of a good education for democracy is to teach about democracy and democratic citizenship comparatively and internationally. The worldwide spread of democracy suggests the need for globalising and internationalising the curriculum in schools. We cannot justify in the United States of America, in the countries of Southeastern Europe, or in any other country an education for democracy that is restricted in scope to a particular sovereign state. If we would teach democracy in schools realistically and responsibly, then we must teach it globally and internationally. And the main method of teaching and learning is the comparative method of analysis and appraisal. By teaching democracy comparatively, we broaden and deepen what students learn.

Breadth of knowledge comes from studying comparatively the wide range of institutional and constitutional designs and political practices across many different democracies of our world. Depth of knowledge about particular principles and institutions of democracy is conveyed by examination of various examples from different countries, which represent variations on the common themes or principles by which we distinguish democratic and undemocratic governments. By teaching democracy comparatively, we direct the attention of students to alternatives and the consequences of making particular decisions. And we enable students to understand the common or generic political and civic choices confronted by people across the cultures and civilisations of our world.

By teaching democracy comparatively, we develop among students a useful method of inquiry that helps them to more readily and accurately understand ideas and information about government, politics, and other aspects of human societies and cultures. By using the comparative method students, can develop high-level intellectual skills. They learn, for example, how to organise and interpret information in terms of categories or concepts, to compare and contrast information according to certain categories or standards, and to make appraisals or evaluations of objects according to particular criteria. Thus, to teach democracy comparatively is to prompt students to think analytically and critically about the constitutions, governments, and political activities of people around the world.

There are three main types of comparisons that teachers and students should make in their global and international studies of democracy.

First, they should use warranted categories as criteria by which to distinguish a democracy from a nondemocracy.

Second, they should use justifiable categories (concepts) to compare and contrast various democratic countries and thereby to appraise the extent to which particular countries are more or less democratic.

Third, they should compare and contrast the constitutions, institutions, and participation of citizens in various democratic countries to understand the different ways that democracy is practiced throughout the world.

The tenth essential element of a good education for democracy is the effective preparation of teachers in terms of the knowledge, skills, and virtues of democratic citizenship. Education for democracy should be brought substantially into university-based programmes of teacher education. It is reasonable to presume that if desirable civic education reforms in primary and secondary schools would succeed, then teachers must be well-prepared to teach democracy and democratic citizenship.

The IEA Civic Education Study revealed that most teachers involved in this international inquiry believed that one very important way to improve education for democracy in schools would be to provide more teacher preparation in the core ideas of democracy and democratic citizenship. And the acclaimed report issued recently, The Civic Mission of Schools, recommended strongly that departments of education in colleges and universities should strengthen the civics components of the pre-service preparation of teachers and the inservice or professional development of teachers in elementary and secondary schools.

Important higher-education reforms in civic education for prospective teachers are being carried out now in several post-communist countries in the Civitas International Exchange Programme conducted by the Center for Civic Education. For example, there are very important programmes on civic learning in teacher preparation in Samara, Russia, in Szeged, Hungary, and in Vilnius, Lithuania. If the preceding elements of a good education for democracy would be carried out successfully in schools, then prospective teachers must be educated in terms of these essential elements; because no one can teach certain knowledge, skills, and virtues to students if she or he has not learned them.

4

Civic Education in Schools

Sound thinking about both education and schooling is impossible unless we clearly distinguish the broader agencies of education from the specific instrument of the school. Unfortunately, advocates of civic education are rarely clear about this fundamental distinction. That we frequently use the word "education" to mean merely schooling-as when we refer to the cost of education or the education budget-doesn't help.

Indeed, "education" has largely become a rhetorically elevated way of referring to mundane schooling. By thus equating education with mere schooling, advocates of civic schooling help themselves to all the rhetorical prestige of civic education. Who can be against civic education? As advocates of civic education frequently point out, since the civic virtues are not innate, they must be learned. And from this true premise they then falsely conclude that civic virtue must be learned in school. If we understand education to refer broadly to all kinds of learning experiences, then it becomes clear that little of our learning takes place in school, but instead takes place at home, among peers, from the media, on the job, at the library, and in places of worship.

Even if we understand education to refer more narrowly to deliberate instruction, then we still can see that school teachers are only one of the many teachers in our lives: clearly our parents are teachers, as are our ministers, coaches, and doctors; our friends often act as teachers, as do journalists, employers, judges, and scout-leaders. So most of our learning is not in school, and most of our teachers are not school teachers. We cannot begin to think clearly about education until we consider the proper role of the school in the context of all the other important modes of education. We might then be able to ask and perhaps answer the questions: of all the places in which we learn, what kind of learning is best suited to the formal school?

Of all the things different people teach us, what kinds of things ought school teachers teach? Rather than just assume that civic education must take place in schools, we are then liberated to consider many other contexts in which we might learn civic virtue and the many other teachers who might lead us to it. We will need to think creatively about other modes of civic education because of what our empirical research tells us about the effectiveness of schools. Since our public schools have a long and pervasive history of engaging in civic education, political scientists over the past five decades have attempted to answer basic questions such as:

Where do citizens acquire their civic knowledge, skills, and virtues? What role do schools play in that acquisition? And, in particular, what role do high school civics courses play? Unfortunately, it is difficult to summarise the findings of the leading researchers about the sources of civic education because some researchers focus on civic skills, some on civic knowledge, and some on civic attitudes, values, and motivations. Those studies focusing on the acquisition of civic competence or civic skills find, not surprisingly, that these skills are mainly acquired not by children in schools, but by adults in churches, unions, civic organisations, and workplaces.

According to these researchers, schools foster civic skills, not by directly teaching civics, but by encouraging students to volunteer in extracurricular organisations and to participate in student government. But even if civic skills are not acquired in schools, surely civic knowledge and civic attitudes might be. After all, there is a long-standing consensus among researchers that the civic knowledge and civic attitudes of an individual are best predicted by his or her years of schooling. For example, M. Kent Jennings and Richard Niemi survey a huge body of literature about the role of education in political socialisation. They report a broad consensus that interest in politics, the possession of political skills, political participation, and support for the liberal democratic creed, all increase with years of schooling. Does this suggest that schools are effectively teaching civic virtue?

Actually, there is no agreement about how to explain the simple correlation between educational attainment and civic virtue. Since years of schooling correlates strongly with parental intelligence, education, and socio-economic status as well as with a student's own intelligence, and subsequent socio-economic status and occupation, it is very difficult to tease out the independent role of schooling. Perhaps some third factor, such as parental education or the student's own intelligence, causes both high educational attainment and civic virtue? Some researchers have found that schooling indirectly shapes political knowledge and attitudes by sorting students into various socio-economic ranks, each with its own distinctive political culture.

Other researchers found that in addition to sorting students into socio-economic ranks, schools also enhance the cognitive sophistication of students and that this greater cognitive sophistication fosters civic knowledge and more tolerant civic attitudes. The sheer cognitive and verbal sophistication fostered by schools seems to indirectly promote certain political attitudes: for example, a college education, especially in the liberal arts, seems to contribute to greater support for the liberal democratic creed. But this effect could not be traced to any particular curriculum or even pedagogical style.

Thus schooling, by fostering greater verbal and cognitive sophistication, also seems to indirectly foster greater civic knowledge and greater political tolerance. But can schools directly impart civic knowledge and proper civic attitudes and motives through a curriculum in civic education? Most states in the U.S. require public schools to teach civics courses. Since advocates of civic education in public schools strongly support such courses, we must ask: what role do civics courses play in fostering desirable political knowledge, attitudes, and conduct?

After a series of studies in the 1960s, Kenneth Langton and M. Kent Jennings published a very influential one focused on the effects of high school civics courses on a range of political knowledge, attitudes, values, and interests. They found that the high school civics curriculum had very little effect on any aspect of political knowledge or values: "Our findings certainly do not support the thinking of those who look to the civics curriculum in American high schools as even a minor source of political socialisation."

In 1974, Langton, Jennings, and Niemi revised and enlarged their original study. They now found that the educational level of parents and the amount of political discourse at home had a much greater impact on the measured knowledge and values than did high school courses; where high school civics courses had any effect, it was only on those students who were just finishing those courses. A subsequent study by Paul Allen Beck and Jennings reconfirmed the impotence of civics courses but found that participation in extracurricular activities, both in high school and beyond, fosters later political participation in young adults.

These and other studies created a lasting professional consensus that the scholastic curriculum in general has some effects on the knowledge but little or no effect on the values, of students and that civics courses in particular have no effect on political knowledge or values. Richard Niemi and Jane Junn challenge this consensus in their major new study, Civic Education: What Makes Students Learn. They analyse data that enables them to study the effects of different kinds of civics courses on students' political knowledge and attitudes. They hypothesise that certain kinds of teaching methods might significantly add or subtract from learning about politics. They found that, although the civics curriculum had much less effect on political knowledge and values than did the home environment, civics courses did matter.

In particular, civics courses that were taken quite recently, had a large variety of topics studied, and included discussion of current events, fostered significantly greater political knowledge. As with earlier studies, they found that although the curriculum had some effect on political knowledge, it had virtually no effect on political attitudes. It is too soon to tell if this new study will alter the existing consensus that civics courses do not matter; some early reviews suggest that consensus is likely to prevail. Indeed, since the Langton and Jennings study was focused on civic attitudes while the Niemi and Junn study was focused on civic knowledge, both studies converge on the qualified conclusion that civics courses have some small effect on civic knowledge but virtually none on civic attitudes.

For those who look to schools as nurseries of civic virtue it is deeply puzzling to note that although we Americans have become vastly more schooled over the past half-century we are also vastly less likely to vote or otherwise participate in politics or civic life. Our hugely increased scholastic attainments have accompanied broad declines in civic virtue and, perhaps even more surprising, no increases in civic knowledge. We ought not be surprised by the evidence that civic virtue is not acquired by children in school. After all, our contemporary political scientists have merely ratified the wisdom of the greatest political philosophers, ancient and modern, who insisted that civic virtue is acquired only by adults from active participation in public affairs.

Plato's guardians, for example, must wait until they are thirty-five years old to begin their fifteen years of civic education, which takes place not in school but in direct participation in governmental affairs. Aristotle is also clear that "a youth is not a suitable student of political science" because, although the intellectual virtues can be taught, the moral virtues result from habit.

For Aristotle, civic education is the responsibility of the legislator, not the teacher: the legislator uses law to educate citizens by insuring that they acquire the right habits as they grow up. Once citizens have grown up with the right civic virtues, then, as mid-career politicians, they might benefit from Aristotle's teaching about politics. Tocqueville beautifully captured the ancient view that schools foster academic knowledge just as politics fosters civic virtue: "The institutions of a township are to freedom what primary schools are to science; they put it within the reach of the people; they make them taste its peaceful employ and habituate them to making use of it."

What we find, then, in Plato, Aristotle, and Tocqueville are very sophisticated analyses of the various agencies of civic education and a conception of civic education that does not rely on the institution of the school. Both political philosophers and political scientists seem to agree, then, that deliberate instruction aimed at inculcating civic knowledge and virtue is strikingly ineffective. Some knowledge of the structure and functions of government might well be taught in civics courses, but not proper civic attitudes, such as a desire to contribute to the common good, a respect for democratic values, a love of country, or toleration of opposed views.

Yet advocates of civic education in schools insist that civic education must aim not just at knowledge but also at civic virtue. Naturally, advocates of civic education are free to insist that although existing methods of teaching civic virtue in schools are ineffective, some new and better kind of civics might work. Still, in the face of existing research, to advocate civic education in schools is the perfect triumph of hope over experience. At the same time, those of us who object to the whole endeavor of using public schools as instruments of partisan civic indoctrination may take some comfort in its near total failure.

Civic Virtue

Curiously, leading contemporary advocates of civic education in schools admit that it is ineffective. What drives the passion for civic and other kinds of moral education is not the conviction that they are effective but the conviction that without civic and moral education, schooling lacks any compelling moral purpose. It is no accident, then, that advocates of civic education in public schools all share the fundamental assumption that purely academic education consists only of the acquisition of skills and information and thus lacks an inherent moral dimension.

If academic education merely involves the acquisition of amoral information and skills-if it is merely about the 3 R's-then we might well ask: "why should any society make a fundamental and expensive public commitment to common schools?" The view that academic education involves the mere acquisition of amoral information and skills is powerfully expressed by Immanuel Kant. Because academic instruction aims only at amoral skills, says Kant, no amount of academic learning can contribute to moral goodness. Arguing that it would be immoral to arm students with powerful intellectual weapons without any guidance about their use, Kant insists upon the need for a supplemental moral education, so that information and skills are put to good moral ends.

By creating a moral vacuum in academic education, Kant has created an urgent need for a compensatory moral education. Ever since Kant, most modern pedagogues have argued over the relative importance of information and skill in academic education, but almost all describe it solely in these amoral terms. Today, for example, Howard Gardner emphasises the acquisition of disciplinary skills while E.D. Hirsch, Jr. emphasises the acquisition of a shared body of information; both of these leading pedagogues agree with Kant that academic education does not itself contribute to moral goodness. What is wrong with this understanding of schooling as a combination of academic skills and moral virtues?

Since the moral virtues on this account have no intrinsic relation to academic excellence in the sense that they are not prerequisites, parts, or consequences of academic excellence, the moral virtues become irrelevant, ancillary or even subversive of, that academic excellence. What do patriotism, courage, tolerance, and temperance have to do with excellence in algebra, history, chemistry, English, and physics?

If academic education intrinsically lacked a compelling moral purpose, thus our students need a compensatory moral education-and an education in the civic virtues might well be the most apt kind in a pluralistic democracy. But, as every good teacher knows, mere information and skills cannot be the aim of academic education because apart from a virtuous orientation toward truth, information and skills are mere resources and tools that can be put into the service of sophistry, manipulation, and domination. Only when the acquisition of information and skills is combined with a proper desire for true knowledge, do we begin to acquire intellectual virtue, which may be defined as the conscientious pursuit of truth.

John Dewey thought that the aim of academic pedagogy was the inculcation of certain traits in students, among them openmindedness, single-mindedness, sincerity, breadth of outlook, thoroughness, and responsibility. Dewey insisted that these academic or intellectual virtues "are moral traits. "Once we grant that academic education is itself a limited kind of moral education, then the question we face is not whether to pursue moral education in schools: academic schooling is intrinsically a kind of moral education. The question we face is rather: what kind of moral education is appropriate to the institution of the school?

Schools seem apt instruments for some, but not all, kinds of moral education. And, we ask: is civic education compatible with the intrinsic moral aim of academic schooling, namely, the conscientious pursuit of true knowledge? As we shall see, civic education, both in theory and in practice, subverts the intrinsic moral purpose of academic schooling. What happens to academic education in the context of schools committed to civic education? Whether we look to the history of civic education or to the ideas of civic educators, the answer is quite certain: the academic pursuit of knowledge will be corrupted through a subordination of truth-seeking to some civic agenda.

The history of civic education in the United States is a cautionary tale indeed. Many advocates of civic education rightly invoke the prestige of Thomas Jefferson, who was a leading pioneer and prophet of using common schools for republican civic education. What these advocates fail to notice, however, is how Jefferson's commitment to civic education corrupted his own intellectual integrity. Jefferson's initial vision of his proposed new University of Virginia reflected his lifelong commitment to the freedom of the human mind from every tyranny erected over it: "This institution," he wrote, "will be based on the illimitable freedom of the human mind.

For here we are not afraid to follow the truth wherever it may lead, nor to tolerate any error so long as reason is left free to combat it. "But as a civic educator Jefferson could not bear the thought of future students at his University being exposed to and corrupted by politically incorrect ideas. Thus, in order to protect them from the seductive Toryism of David Hume, Jefferson spent two decades promoting the publication of a censored, plagiarised, and falsified but politically correct edition of Hume's History of England. When he could find no partners in this intellectual crime, he then enlisted James Madison's support as a fellow member of the Board of Overseers of the nascent University of Virginia to draft regulations aimed at suppressing political heresy and promoting political orthodoxy.

Jefferson and Madison succeeded in passing a resolution to "provide that none [of the principles of government] shall be inculcated which are incompatible with those on which the Constitutions of this state, and of the US. were genuinely based, in the common opinion..." This resolution goes on to specify the texts that must be taught in the school of politics (Locke, Sidney, The Federalist, and U.S. and Virginia constitutional documents). Moreover, Jefferson came to agree with Madison's argument that "the most effectual safeguard against heretical intrusions into the School of politics, will be an able & orthodox Professor...". To this end, Jefferson and later Madison worked to ensure that only those professors who espoused a strict construction of the U.S. constitution and the doctrine of states' rights would be appointed to the school of politics.

Because of his passion for civic education in republican virtue, Jefferson abandoned his commitment to intellectual freedom in favour of partisan indoctrination at his own beloved University of Virginia. That such a champion of intellectual freedom who swore undying enmity to every tyranny over the mind of man should himself attempt to whitewash, censor, and suppress what he called "heresy" powerfully illustrates the poisonous consequences of using schools as instruments of civic education.

Jefferson has truly been the poisoned well-spring of American civic education in schools ever since. Some historians have systematically analysed the civic values taught in public school civics, literature, history, and social studies courses. It should be no surprise that in order to teach civic values, American textbook writers in every epoch have systematically sanitised, distorted, and falsified history, literature, and social studies in order to inculcate racism, nationalism, every manner of religious, cultural and class bigotry, Anglo-Saxon superiority, American imperialism, Social Darwinism, anti- Catholicism, and anti-intellectualism.

An early text from 1796 warns of the danger posed by the importation of French ideas and persons: "Let America beware of infidelity, which is the most dangerous enemy that she has to contend with at present..."; the author goes on to teach school children that Native Americans lack all science, culture and religion, that they are averse to labour and foresight, and that "the beavers exceed the Indians, ten-fold, in the construction of their homes and public works...". Later, in the wake of large-scale Irish immigration, school texts began a massive campaign of slander and calumny against Roman Catholicism. Textbooks not only describe Catholicism as an anti-Christian form of paganism and idolatry, they even blame the Church for the fall of the Roman Empire. One speller asks: "Is papacy at variance with paganism?"

A historian says that no theme in school texts before 1870 is more universal than anti- Catholicism; according to these texts, Catholicism has no place in the American past or future. In the period after 1870, religious bigotry gives way to racial bigotry and all non-Anglo-Saxon peoples are described as permanently and immutably inferior due to their intellectual, moral, and physical degeneracy. Beginning in 1917, many states began to pass laws forbidding any instruction in public schools that might be disloyal to the United States, including the teaching of the German language; at the same time, many states also passed laws requiring all public schoolteachers to be American citizens and to swear an oath that they will teach patriotism.

Nor is this subordination of knowledge to civic uplift a relic of the past: in many states, creationism is taught in place of biology and geology because of the perceived moral dangers of Darwinism. And many states continue to require American history to be falsified in order to promote patriotism: the Texas Education Code provides that "textbooks should promote democracy, patriotism, and the free enterprise system"; this provision is still employed to sanitise the teaching of history in Texas. The New York Board of Regents was found to have falsified, on moral grounds, most of the literary texts used in its exams; here classic literature was bowdlerised in the interests of political correctness.

Some systematic studies of current social studies and history textbooks find extensive evidence of how American history is now distorted, twisted, and falsified in order to emphasise the previously neglected contributions as well as the victimisation of women and minorities. Although Anglo-Saxon triumphalism now frequently gives way to multicultural victimisation, nothing has changed in the American passion for subordinating truth-seeking to moral and civic uplift.

No one should be surprised that American schoolbooks, like any fallible form of human knowledge, should often prove mistaken and misguided. But our textbooks do not go astray merely because their authors were fallible human beings sincerely seeking true knowledge; rather, these texts go astray because their authors deliberately subordinate the pursuit of knowledge to an agenda for civic education. Our textbooks are often explicitly anti-intellectual: they repeatedly emphasise that moral and civic virtue is far more important than mere knowledge. What again and again proves fatal to the pursuit of knowledge is the conviction that civic virtue is more important than truth.

Indeed, some leading contemporary advocates of civic education in schools frankly admit the need to sanitise and falsify history. Civic education in schools usually involves various kinds of duplicity on the part of educators. For example, teachers pretend to teach American history, but actually use historical examples to covertly impart one or another civic virtue. In response to the traditionally rosy and uplifting versions of American greatness designed to instill patriotism we now find dark and brutal narratives of American imperialism and racism designed to covertly instill multicultural tolerance.

Both conservative and progressive civic educators routinely subordinate the quest for truth to a preferred agenda for civic uplift. In English courses, literature is selected not on the grounds of its beauty, renown, or utility for teaching prose-style, but because it presents desirable moral lessons, such as how boys love to cook.

Civic education poses a profound threat not only to the integrity of the curriculum but also to the integrity of pedagogical techniques. Much of what is known as "progressive" educational pedagogy, that is, teaching that attempts to respond to the spontaneous curiosity of the student, often in hands-on, collaborative projects, has long been advocated on moral and civic grounds as much as on academic grounds. John Dewey, in particular, championed many progressive pedagogical innovations because he thought they turned classrooms into laboratories of democracy.

Progressive pedagogues have always championed their techniques on the grounds that they are egalitarian, democratic, tolerant, caring, and fostering of autonomy. Critics of progressivism have wondered why these methods are so widely adopted when there is so little empirical evidence of their effectiveness. But the passion for progressivism, like the passion for civic education more broadly, does not rest upon the conviction that it is effective but on the conviction that it is morally desirable. Indeed, some advocates of civic education defend progressive pedagogical methods even when they are not academically warranted on the grounds that these methods produce better future citizens.

So civic educators are often quite frank about the need to subordinate not only truth but also academic achievement more broadly to the imperatives of civic virtue. In practice, then, and in theory, we have compelling evidence that civic education poses a fundamental and permanent threat to both the academic curriculum and to academic pedagogy. How seriously we take this subordination of academic to civic education depends upon our understanding of the values and virtues intrinsic to academic education.

Academic education is a kind of moral education is to point out that the information and skills acquired in school are just as easily put in the service of sophistry as in the service of truth-seeking. But this view of academic education in terms of mere information and skills misdescribes the actual point of scholastic education, which is to acquire information and skills in the context of a love for genuine knowledge. In other words, good math, history, science, and English teachers do not attempt to arm students with morally-neutral resources and weapons and then hope for the best.

Good teachers attempt to fuse the growing acquisition of information and skill to a growing desire for genuine knowledge. In other words, proper academic education does not seek merely to provide the means for whatever ends might be chose by the student; proper academic education encompasses both the means and the end. John Dewey saw this clearly: "The knowledge of dynamite of a safecracker may be identical in verbal form with that of a chemist; in fact, it is different, for it is knit into connection with different aims and habits, and thus has a different import."

The aim of academic education is the acquisition of those traits of character, such as thoroughness, accuracy, perseverance, intellectual humility and intellectual courage, that make us conscientious in the pursuit of true knowledge. Our relation to these academic virtues is fundamentally different from our relation to our capacities and skills. Capacities and skills, like any resource or tool, are things we can use or misuse; we recognise a kind of 'distance' between our selves and our capacities or skills. Virtues, however, are not capacities or skills but qualities or aspects of persons: virtues cannot be misused because they cannot be used at all.

Virtues define who we are; they are not things to be employed. Academic education aims not only to equip us with new resources and skills but also to transform us as persons: from persons who have a curiosity for knowledge but who are credulous and prone to false beliefs into persons who love and can reliably acquire genuine knowledge. Academic education is as deep, transformative, and virtuous as any other kind of moral education. What evidence do we have that schools are the proper instrument for academic education?

Empirical studies of civic education found that schools did have some small effect on civic knowledge even if virtually no effect on civic attitudes or virtues. There are no empirical studies of the effectiveness of schools in inculcating the intellectual virtues. But the most influential study of the effects of scholastic attainment on the knowledge of adults may be suggestive of the important role of schools in inculcating not just a body of information but also in fostering a disposition to the lifelong acquisition of knowledge.

Herbert Hyman, Charles Wright, and John Reed in their The Enduring Effects of Education, surveyed the knowledge of adults many decades after they had completed their schooling. They found not only that every year of schooling contributed positively to the knowledge base of adults but also that every year of schooling contributed positively to the propensity of adults to continue learning by reading newspapers, magazines, books, and seeking out opportunities for adult education.

By including in their survey knowledge of current events, these researchers were able to establish that those adults who had the most schooling were also keeping abreast of current events most effectively. So we have some evidence that schools do effectively foster a lifelong love for learning. Once we see that the conscientious pursuit of knowledge is the inherent moral purpose of schooling, we will not be surprised by the absence of any agreement about which civic virtues we ought to teach in schools.

Since none of the civic virtues is intrinsically related to the inherent moral purpose of schooling, there is no academically principled way to decide which civic virtues ought to be taught in schools. No catalogue of civic virtues can be shown to be a prerequisite of academic excellence, a part of academic excellence, or the product of academic excellence.

The simple truth of the matter is that one can be a paragon of academic virtue and a lousy citizen. Many great scholars, scientists, and educators have notoriously lacked the civic virtues by being resident aliens, cosmopolitians, or Epicureans. Trying to decide which civic virtues to teach in schools is like trying to decide which sports or which crafts to teach: since none of these is intrinsically related to academic education, there are no academic grounds for deciding these matters. Because civic education, like driver or consumer education, lacks an intrinsic relation to the academic curriculum, it quickly becomes regarded by teachers and students as ancillary and irrelevant.

The purely ancillary nature of civics courses may help to explain why they prove to be so ineffective. To overcome this irrelevance, many advocates insist that civic education become incorporated into the core academic curriculum, so that English, history, and social studies courses impart lessons in civic virtue. But here we become impaled upon the fundamental dilemma of civic education: if we teach civic virtue in a way that respects the integrity of the academic curriculum, then civics becomes merely ancillary and irrelevant; but if, to overcome this irrelevance, we attempt to incorporate civic education into the academic subjects, then we inevitably subvert the inherent moral aim of those subjects by subordinating the pursuit of truth to civic uplift.

Indeed, there may be something paradoxical and self-defeating about the whole project of teaching civic virtue in schools. Political scientists Niemi and Junn speculate that civic education might be ineffective largely because it is so whitewashed. So instead of a nasty contest between interest groups, we get "how a bill becomes law"-a presentation of civics cleansed of all politics as well of all possible interest. And they also decry the Whiggish distortions of American history, in which the "problems" of the past (such as racism and oppression) are invariably "solved" in the present. Neimi and Junn worry that these attempts to inculcate civic trust might not just be ineffective but actually backfire by creating greater political cynicism. Political theorist Christopher Eisgruber similarly observes of the attempt to inculcate values through an academic course: "How would students react to such a course?

My suspicion is that any student old enough to understand such a course would also be old enough to recognise it as propaganda-and to resent it for that reason. "Students are often adept at detecting when knowledge is treated merely as a vehicle for carrying moral attitudes; these students then rightly suspect the credentials of such knowledge. If a teacher expresses such contempt for the value of the knowledge they teach, why should students value learning it? That civic education aimed directly at civic virtues is ineffective is, in many ways, reassuring. But it would be deeply unfortunate if, as many argue, the attempt to inculcate civic virtues serves to undermine the teaching of civic knowledge.

Instead of constantly subordinating knowledge to moral uplift, we ought to have more confidence in the sheer moral value of knowledge. As we have seen, the sheer cognitive sophistication cultivated in schools strongly contributes to political tolerance, that is, the willingness to extend civil liberties to those with whom we strongly disagree. A leading team of political scientists offer this hypothesis: "If we are correct that the number of years of formal schooling acts to increase tolerance regardless of the manifest and subtle political content of that education, then educational attainment should act to increase tolerance even in regimes with contrary messages." They found strong evidence that years of schooling increased political tolerance even in communist Hungary.

Ironically, intolerant regimes foster toleration simply by schooling their citizens-even when (or especially when?) that schooling is designed to foster political intolerance. And specifically political knowledge has been shown to promote political tolerance, active participation in politics, more coherent political opinions, and a more rational relation between participation and one's political goals. So we ought to be confident that we are contributing significantly to civic virtue merely by attempting to impart genuine knowledge and in particular, civic knowledge, to our students.

In light of the ineffective and often counter-productive nature of civic education aimed directly at civic virtue, we have many reasons to believe that schools are better advised simply to stick to their essential task of pursuing genuine knowledge. No doubt this scholastic kind of civic education is seriously deficient, but we must remember that most of what we learn in life is not learned in school and most of our teachers are not schoolteachers. What is the relation of schooling to civic education more broadly?

A good citizen ought to possess the intellectual virtues because they will help him or her to resist false beliefs; bad politicians frequently tempt us to believe things that are false by appealing to our national pride, our greed, our resentments, or our fears for the future. Intellectual virtue means precisely acquiring those dispositions that lead us to resist these temptations to false beliefs. A good citizen need not care only about the truth of his or her political beliefs; nor must a good citizen, as a partisan, advocate the whole truth. But a good citizen must care about whether the views he or she advocates are true.

So intellectual virtue might be necessary for good citizens but hardly sufficient. An intellectual paragon might well be a lousy citizen: no amount of conscientiousness in the pursuit of truth constitutes or even reliably leads to a zeal for public service or the courage to defend one's nation. Indeed, as Plato famously observed, those who most sincerely love genuine knowledge are often the most repelled by the inevitable simplifications and distortions of political ideology and rhetoric. It is very difficult to reconcile a passion for knowledge with the political imperatives to advocate partial truths, to hide the truth at times, and to appeal to non-rational passions. None of this amounts to a fundamental incompatibility between intellectual and civic virtue but it does suggest some real tensions and moral challenges. So a scholastic education is only a partial civic education and the intellectual virtues are only a part of the civic virtues.

5

Teaching of Democracy

In this century, by contrast with the past, we may reasonably speculate that education for citizenship in a democracy will, with each decade, become everywhere more global, international, and comparative in curricular content and processes of teaching and learning. And we ought to think now about how to improve our current curricular frameworks and standards for a world transformed by globally accepted and internationally transcendent principles and processes of democracy. The forward-looking education for democracy, which we should contemplate, involves globalisation and internationalisation of the curriculum in primary and secondary schools and in university-based programmes for the preparation of teachers.

Following are five propositions that apply equally to preadult education for democratic citizenship and to civic learning in the preparation of teachers.

Proposition 1: At all levels of preadult education and in programmes of teacher preparation, we should teach a global or universal definition of democracy so that students can compare and evaluate regimes according to a common and minimal world standard: The first objective of a good education for democratic citizenship is to teach exactly what a democracy is, and what it is not. If students are to become competent citizens of a democracy, they must know how to distinguish and evaluate types of government. The label democracy has too often been used by despotic regimes with mere showcase constitutions that hypocritically claimed to be exemplars of democracy and freedom. The so-called 'democracies' or 'democratic-republics' of communist countries were and are tragic examples of the bogus use of a political label.

Through their civic education, students should develop defensible criteria by which to think critically and comparatively and thereby to evaluate the extent to which their government and other governments of the world do or do not function authentically as democracies. There is broad international agreement today on a minimal or threshold standard by which to judge whether or not a regime is a democracy. This minimal criterion is the regular occurrence of free, open, fair, and contested elections by which an inclusive citizenry selects its representatives in government. Thus, there is government by consent of the governed in which the people's representatives are accountable to the people. This definition is today's minimal global standard for international recognition of a regime as an electoral democracy.

If there is no viable opposition party to contest elections, or if the right to vote or otherwise participate is systematically denied to particular categories of persons for reasons of race, ethnicity, sexual identity, religion, ideology, and so forth, then there cannot be an authentic electoral democracy. All citizens in a genuine democracy are able to participate fairly, freely, and openly to influence their government by campaigning and voting in public elections and by participating during the periods between regularly scheduled elections to promote personal and group interests and to influence policy decisions by their representatives in government.

The people of the polity, including those outside the momentary majority, must have the political rights to freedom of speech, press, assembly, association, and petition for redress of grievances. And most importantly, parties in loyal opposition to the rulers of the moment must have a fair chance to supplant them in the next election. The acid test or critical rule by which to determine the establishment of an electoral democracy is the orderly transfer of power to govern from one party to another through a legitimate democratic election. If this rule prevails in at least two consecutive elections, then a regime may claim legitimately to be an established electoral democracy.

In 2002, 121 of the world's 192 sovereign states could be recognised as democracies in terms of the minimal global standard for an electoral democracy. The collective populations of these electoral democracies accounted for 64.6% of the world's population. By contrast, in 1900 there was not even one country in the world that met today's minimal global standard for democracy. In 1950, there were only 22 authentic democracies with 14.3% of the world's population. By the end of the 20 century, however, there was a dramatic global trend toward electoral democracy, as communist regimes and other types of autocratic or authoritarian systems withered and died. These data on the worldwide spread of democracy are provided by Freedom House, a greatly respected non governmental organisation in the United States of America.

The global trend toward electoral or minimal democracy has not immediately brought about an equivalent surge toward personal or private rights to freedom. In 2002, according to the annual Freedom House Survey, 85 of the world's 121 electoral democracies were rated 'free,' which means that they maintained a high degree of political, personal, and economic freedom. The 'fully free' countries included 40.8% of the world's population in 2002. The other 36 of the world's electoral democracies were rated 'partly free' because they did not fully protect the private and personal rights of their people.

And 48 countries, with 35.4% of the world's population in 2002, had a rating of 'not free' because they completely denied to their people basic rights of freedom and civil liberties. Among the worst-rated countries in 2002 were the remaining communist regimes: China, Cuba, and North Korea. And among the world's freest countries were such formerly Soviet Socialist Republics as Estonia, Latvia, and Lithuania and such post-communist countries as the Czech Republic, Hungary, and Poland. The most democratic and free regions of the world today are West and East-Central Europe and the Americas. Among the 35 countries in the Americas, 32 are electoral democracies (91 percent). In addition, 22 states are rated as both democratic and fully free (63 percent).

In the fully free democratic countries, protection of individual rights extends beyond minimal protection of political rights to fundamental personal and private rights, such as freedom of conscience, free exercise of religion, unrestricted freedom of association, the secure ownership and use of private property, and security against unwarranted intrusions by government into one's private life. These private rights are not fully guaranteed in the 'partly free' electoral democracies.

Proposition 2: At all levels of preadult education and in programmes of teacher preparation, we should teach a short set of six core concepts by which students can think beyond the minimal global standard for an electoral democracy to compare and evaluate political systems more deeply and complexly: An advanced or more fully developed conceptualisation of democracy in today's world includes electoral and representative democracy in concert with the rule of law/ limited government, human rights, citizenship, civil society, and market economy. A polity that embodies the six core concepts in Table 1 is properly labelled a constitutional representative democracy or a constitutional democratic-republic, and it paradoxically provides majority rule with equal protection of the public and private rights of all persons in the polity.

Table 1: Concepts at the Core of a Global Education for Democracy

1. Representative democracy (republicanism)
   - a. Popular sovereignty (government by consent of the governed, the people)
   - b. Representation and accountability in a government of, by, and for the people
   - c. Free, fair, and competitive elections of representatives in government
   - d. Comprehensive eligibility to participate freely to vote and campaign in elections
   - e. Inclusive and free political participation for personal and common interests
   - f. Majority rule of the people for the common good
2. Rule of law (constitutionalism)
   - a. Rule of law in the government, society, and economy
   - b. A government limited and empowered to secure human rights and maintain order
   - c. Equality, liberty, and justice under law
   - d. Separation and sharing of powers as a means to limited government
   - e. An independent judiciary, power of judicial/constitutional review

f. Negative and positive constitutionalism

3. Human rights (liberalism)
    - a. Natural rights/constitutional rights to liberty, equality, and justice
    - b. Political or public rights
    - c. Personal or private rights
    - d. Economic, social, cultural, and environmental rights
    - e. Rights associated with negative and positive constitutionalism
    - f. Individual and collective rights
4. Citizenship (civism)
    - a. Membership in a people based on legal qualifications of citizenship
    - b. Rights, responsibilities, and roles of citizenship
    - c. Civic identity
    - d. Citizenship in a unitary, federal, confederal, or consociational system
    - e. Means and ends of political and civic participation
5. Civil society (communitarianism)
    - a. Voluntary membership in nongovernmental organisations or civil associations
    - b. Freedom of association, assembly, and social choice
    - c. Pluralism, multiple and overlapping group memberships and identities
    - d. Social regulation for the common good (rule of law, traditions, morals)
    - e. Civic participation for personal interests and the common good
    - f. Free and open social system
6. Market economy (capitalism)
    - a. Freedom of exchange and economic choice through the market
    - b. Protection of private property rights
    - c. Freedom to own and use property for personal gain and the public good

d. Economic regulation for the common good (rule of law, traditions, morals)

e. Free and open economic system

Acquisition of the six core concepts as a set, a framework of connected ideas, enables learners to know complexly and deeply what a fully developed democracy in today's world is, and what it is not; to distinguish the advanced form of democracy from other types of government, including less developed democracies; and to evaluate the extent or degree to which their government and other governments of the world are or are not authentic constitutional representative democracies.

Representative Democracy and Constitutionalism: Republicanism or representative democracy, the first core concept in the list of six, entails the minimal electoral standard. The second concept of this list, the rule of law or constitutionalism, is the key to the entire set of concepts in Table 1. Constitutionalism means limited government and the rule of law to prevent the arbitrary use of power, to protect human rights, to regulate democratic procedures in elections and public policy making, and to achieve a community's shared purposes. Constitutionalism in a democracy, therefore, both limits and empowers government of, by, and for the people.

Through a constitution to which they have consented, the people grant power to the government to act effectively for the common good. The people also set constitutional limits on the power of their democratic government in order to prevent tyranny and to protect their rights. So, in an authentic constitutional democratic-republic, the people's elected representatives in government are limited by the supreme law of the people's constitution for the primary purposes of protecting equally the rights of everyone in the polity and thereby promoting the common good of the community.

Human Rights, Constitutionalism, and Democracy: Through a comparative and international education for democratic citizenship, students should learn the close connection between constitutionalism and human rights in a democracy. (Table 1.) Constitutional limitations on the government's power are necessary to guarantee political rights necessary to the conduct of free, fair, open, and periodic competitive elections by the people of their representatives in government. In a democracy, there must be no possibility for rulers to punish, incarcerate, or destroy their political opponents.

Finally, constitutionalism involves limitation on the power of the majority to prevent unjust treatment of individuals in the minority. An ultimate test of constitutionally guaranteed freedom in any country of the world is the extent to which the least popular groups and individuals are able to exercise and enjoy their rights on equal terms with others in the polity. If there truly is equal protection of human rights, then there really is a fully free constitutional democracy. Otherwise, there may be tyranny of the majority or democratic despotism, but not equal liberty and justice under law. Through comparative analysis and appraisal of regimes, students can judge for themselves the extent to which different governments meet the criteria for becoming and being both democratic and free and avoiding majority tyranny, the malady of a democracy that does not have sufficient constitutional limits on the government's exercise of power.

Citizenship, Constitutionalism, and Democracy: The source of constitutional authority in a democracy is the people, who are the citizens of the polity. (Table 1.) The citizens agree collectively to consent to the supreme law of a constitution. They consent to limit their collective exercise of power to guarantee the freedom of everyone in the polity. Thus, democracy is limited constitutionally to protect freedom against the threat of majority tyranny. A primary and continual question in the origin and evolution of a democracy is: who, exactly, are the people? The constitutional answer to this question determines who will or will not be a citizen, a full and equal member of a democratic political and civic community, such as a country or nation-state.

So citizenship in a democracy, just like guarantees of human rights, is rooted in constitutionalism. The status of citizenship involves very important obligations and responsibilities, such as paying taxes, serving in the country's armed forces when called upon, obeying laws enacted by one's representatives in government, demonstrating commitment and loyalty to the democratic political community and state, constructively criticizing the conditions of political and civic life, and participating to improve the quality of political and civic life. Citizenship in a constitutional representative democracy provides those who share it with common cords of political loyalty and civic identity. Citizenship is connected variously to a popularly ratified constitution in different democracies of our world.

Democratic countries can be judged more or less free depending on how extensively and equally the rights and responsibilities of citizenship are distributed among the people of the polity. Thus, students involved in education for democratic citizenship need to study comparatively and internationally what citizenship is in different countries, how it is acquired or lost in various political systems, what rights and responsibilities are entailed by it, how it is connected to the institutions of particular nation-states, especially their own, and how it is exercised similarly and differently throughout the world.

Civil Society, Constitutionalism, and Democracy: Civic participation, a right and responsibility of democratic citizenship, is exercised through the voluntary associations of civil society, which is a country's network of freely formed associations. (Table 1.) Distinct from the formal governmental institutions of the state, private civil associations may act independently or cooperatively with state agencies to promote the common good. But they may also act as an independent social force to check or limit an abusive or undesired exercise of the state's power.

Civil society can be a counter vailing force against the state to oppose despotism and protect the civil liberties and rights of individuals and groups. Apart from the state, but subject to the rule of law in a constitution, civil society is a public domain that private individuals create and operate to strengthen their communities and advance their personal and collective interests. Examples of non governmental organisations that constitute civil society are free labour unions, religious communities, human-rights advocacy groups, environmental protection organisations, support groups providing social welfare services to needy people, independent newspaper and magazine publishing houses, independent and private schools, and professional associations.

An individual of a free country may belong to many civil society organisations at once and throughout a lifetime. Civil society organisations in pursuit of the common good are a manifestation of community solidarity or communitarianism. As such, civil society provides protection from anomie and radical individualism. And it is both a buffer and conduit between the state and the citizen, which protects human rights against state-based despotism and provides channels for organised expression of community needs or grievances. Finally, civil society organisations provide rich and varied opportunities for civic participation that enable citizens to learn democracy by doing it and to develop social capital (resources and competencies) that make a democracy functional and sustainable.

Students should be taught to distinguish democratic from non democratic governments by using as a criterion the idea of civil society. The vitality of civil society is a gauge of the strength and prospects of democracy in any country of the world. By contrast, genuine civil society organisations cannot exist in a totalitarian regime, which attempts to control the people through an unlimited one-party government. Thus, if students would comparatively know, analyse, and appraise democracy in their country or elsewhere, they must be able to comprehend the idea of civil society, to assess the activities of civil society organisations, and to connect their knowledge of civil society to other core concepts, such as constitutionalism, human rights, and citizenship. (Table 1.)

Market Economy, Constitutionalism, and Democracy: A dynamic civil society interacts with a market economy, a form of capitalism which involves competition and freedom of exchange at the marketplace. The market is the free and open space where buyers and sellers choose to exchange goods and services. Market-based capitalism involves private ownership and use for profit of the means of production, distribution, and exchange of goods and services. (Table 1.) Both the market economy and the civil society are free and open systems through which information, ideas, and products are exchanged for personal gain and the public good. Economic competition and exchange at the market, like other social interactions of a constitutional representative democracy, are regulated by the state through the rule of law, which provides the order and stability necessary to guarantee individual rights to life, liberty, property, equality of opportunity, and so forth.

So, freedom of economic and social activity in an authentic democracy is the consequence of constitutionalism. According to an eminent political scientist, Robert Dahl, '[D]emocracy has existed only in countries with predominately market-capitalist economies and never (or at most briefly) in countries with predominately non market economies'. A freely functioning market checks concentrations of power in government that could be exercised against human rights. In tandem with a free and open civil society, capitalism and the market enable development and maintenance of plural sources of power to counteract the power of the state and safeguard the people's freedoms of expression, assembly, association, and so forth.

A centrally directed command economy, the antithesis of the market economy, substitutes the directives of government officials with virtually unlimited state power for the free choices and competition of the marketplace. Through their total control of the production and distribution of goods and services (wealth and the means to acquire wealth), the government officials in command of the economy have power to control totally the inhabitants in their realm. There are no effective limits on their power to abuse individuals at odds with the state or to deprive unpopular persons of their rights to liberty, to equality of opportunity, and to life.

Education for democratic citizenship should emphasise the necessary connection of capitalism and a market economy to civil society. Students should learn that there can be no advanced or fully free democracy without civil society, and there can be no civil society without a market economy. Further, they should understand that both a market economy and civil society depend upon constitutionalism. There cannot be an authentically free society and free economy without constitutionally based regulation for the common good. Finally, education for democratic citizenship should involve students in comparative and international studies of relationships between constitutional governments, civil societies, and market economies.

A perennial global issue in all constitutional democracies of our world pertains to how much and what kind of legal regulation there should be. Fundamental rights of individuals will be at risk if there is too much regulation or too little regulation by the constitutional government. Achieving the appropriate mixture of liberty and order, freedom and regulation, is a challenge faced by citizens of every democracy. Thus, comparative analyses of issues about the extent and kind of governmental economic and social regulations in different democratic countries should be part of education for democratic citizenship.

Proposition 3: At all levels of preadult education and in programmes of teacher preparation, we should use the set of six core concepts on the meaning and practice of democracy to structure comparative and international inquiry about constitutions, governmental institutions, human rights, and participation in the democracies of our world: The six core concepts in Table 1 are common themes or attributes of all genuine democracies. However, the constitutional designs and institutional structures of different countries are variations on the common core concepts or themes. They are alternative ways to put the common themes or concepts into practice. For example, the separation and sharing of power in government is a common characteristic of constitutionalism in all democracies of our world. However, there are alternative ways to practice this necessary attribute of democratic constitutional design.

The American model of constitutional representative democracy distributes power among three coordinate branches of government: the legislative, executive, and judicial departments. Each branch has constitutional means to check the actions of the other branches to prevent any of the three coordinate branches from continually dominating or controlling the others. These constitutional checks involve practical overlapping and sharing of powers among three distinct branches of the government, each with a particular function. Of course, the American model is merely one way to separate, distribute, and share power in constitutional government.

There are other workable structures, such as those associated with various forms of the parliamentary type of constitutional democracy. The parliamentary democracies usually exemplify legislative primacy vis-à-vis the executive functions of government. However, they also tend to have a separate and truly independent judiciary, usually including a constitutional court with the power of constitutional review, which is roughly similar to the judicial review of the American system. For example, the three Baltic States of Estonia, Latvia, and Lithuania are parliamentary democracies with constitutional courts that exercise the power of constitutional review. A notable worldwide trend in constitutionalism has been the distribution to an in dependent judiciary of the power to declare legislative and executive acts unconstitutional. This is a critical constitutional means to stop the legislative and executive powers from being used to violate human rights or subvert democracy.

A bill of rights in a constitution may eloquently declare lofty words about rights to life, liberty, property, and various forms of social security. But these rights will be practically useless unless there is governmental machinery to enforce them against acts of despotism or neglect. The constitutional courts of parliamentary democracies only respond to constitutional questions. Issues that pertain strictly to statutory interpretation, apart from the constitutionality of a law, usually are resolved by other courts, without action by the constitutional court. Unlike the American judiciary, these constitutional courts may provide opinions about the constitutionality of an act apart from the adversary process whereby a real case involving the act at issue is brought before the court by a prosecutor or someone filing suit against another party. Thus, these constitutional courts may render advisory opinions, which is not done by the American judiciary.

The essence of constitutional review by the constitutional courts, however, is the same as judicial review in the United States. Another fundamental aspect of comparative constitutionalism in education for democracy pertains to different kinds of constitutional guarantees for human rights. In the United States of America, there has been a long-standing tradition of inherent or 'unalienable' natural rights. Thus, in the American political tradition the constitutional government is expected to be the guarantor and protector of God-given rights possessed equally by each person prior to the establishment of the government. Indeed, the 1776 Declaration of Independence proclaims that 'governments are instituted among men to secure these rights.' So, in the United States, there has been a long-standing tradition against the idea that rights are granted by the government.

By contrast, the tradition of legal positivism prevails in the constitutions of many democracies in the world. In the Constitution of Latvia, for example, Article 89, states that rights are recognised and guaranteed only 'in accordance with this Constitution, laws and international agreements binding upon Latvia'. The idea of negative constitutionalism is embedded in the Constitution of the United States. Thus, there are provisions in this Constitution that specifically prohibit the government from denying or abusing the natural rights of individuals. Negative constitutionalism is exemplified by Amendments 1-10 of the U.S. Constitution, which are commonly called the Bill of Rights. These amendments are directed against the power of government to stop it from depriving an individual of her or his civil liberties.

Amendment I of the U.S. Constitution's Bill of Rights, for example, says, 'Congress shall make no law respecting an establishment of religion, or prohibiting the free exercise thereof; or abridging the freedom of speech, or of the press, or the right of the people peaceably to assemble, and to petition the Government for a redress of grievances'. Restrictions on the power of government to protect rights to liberty can be found in the constitution of every state in the world that is committed to constitutional democracy. For example, the kinds of rights guaranteed in the U.S. Bill of Rights can be found in the constitutions of Estonia, Latvia, and Lithuania. So, all democratic countries practice negative constitutionalism as a means to guarantee certain human rights.

By contrast with the U.S. Constitution, however, the constitutions of Estonia and Lithuania also exemplify positive constitutionalism in regard to human rights; this means that the government is constitutionally directed to act affirmatively to provide certain social and economic rights to individuals. For example, the 1992 Constitution of Lithuania says in Article 41, 'Citizens who demonstrate suitable progress should be guaranteed education at establishments of higher education free of charge.' And in Articles 52 and 53 there are guarantees of rights to social, economic, and medical benefits: 'The state shall guarantee the right of citizens to old age and disability pension, as well as to social assistance in the event of unemployment, sickness, widowhood, loss of the breadwinner.... The state shall take care of people's health, and shall guarantee medical aid to citizens free of charge at state medical facilities....'.

Unlike the United States Constitution, positive constitutionalism in regard to rights is found in most constitutions of the world's democracies. In some constitutions, the guarantees of social, economic, cultural, and environmental rights are very great in number and broad in scope to the point of empowering the government to very amply intrude into the private lives of citizens and the operations of the civil society and economy to redistribute resources or otherwise promote social and economic equality of the citizenry. In the United States, social and economic rights are not constitutionalised. Rather, social and economic rights are provided more or less through the legislative process. Thus, they may be expanded or narrowed or even eliminated through the enactment of laws. But they are not guaranteed by the Constitution.

Education for democratic citizenship should include lessons that require students to examine, compare, and evaluate human rights claims on government, which exemplify both negative and positive constitutionalism.

And these lessons should involve comparative analysis and appraisal by students about alternative viewpoints concerning negative and positive constitutionalism and the extent to which social and economic rights should be guaranteed by a constitutional democracy. Through these lessons students should comprehend that availability of resources enables or limits a government's capacity to guarantee certain social and economic rights. Further, they should examine the possible threats to liberty that come from empowering a government beyond certain limits, even in the cause of equality, justice, and the common good. Insufficient limitations on the exercise of positive constitutionalism could lead directly to the possibility of despotism or even totalitarianism of the kind exercised by the discredited and defunct government of the Soviet Union.

A basic human right in a constitutional representative democracy is political participation, which is a means for citizens to influence public decisions and resolve public issues. In a democracy, voting in public elections is the typical type of political participation. But involvement in the activities of a political party, in the work of a political interest group, or in a public protest movement are other common forms of participation by citizens in a democracy. Political participation in an autocratic or totalitarian regime may be extensive, but it is by command of the state. By contrast, political participation in a constitutional democracy is uncoerced by the state and its rulers, and it is limited legitimately only by the rule of law, which is anchored in the consent of the people. Education for democracy should include comparative analysis of the extent and types of political participation in democratic and non democratic systems.

For example, students should learn now citizens participate in political parties and how participation in voting and elections varies in a two-party system, such as the United States and the United Kingdom, by contrast with a multi-party system, such as India and Italy. The key point, however, is to note that like other generic characteristics of democracy, there is variation on the common theme of participation by citizens in the different democracies of the world. But there is an authentic democracy only when there is relatively unfettered freedom of citizens to participate in elections and between elections to influence decisions of the government.

Through comparative and international inquiries, students of democracy should compare and assess the extent and methods of participation as a means to influence government in their country and in other countries. However, if students would be engaged most productively in comparative lessons about constitutions, institutions, human rights, and participation, then they need a core curriculum that conjoins interactively the knowledge, skills, and dispositions that constitute competent citizenship in any authentic democracy of our contemporary world.

Proposition 4: At all levels of preadult education and in programmes of teacher preparation, we should provide a global, international, and comparative education for democracy in terms of four connected and interactive components or categories: civic knowledge, cognitive civic skills, participatory civic skills, and civic dispositions: The four components of education for democracy are congruent with teaching and learning the six core concepts by which we define, compare, and evaluate democratic and non democratic governments.

Civic knowledge, however, is primary. Content not process should be the foundation of the curriculum. Good comparative, international, and global education for democracy is anchored in civic knowledge. It emphasises deep and abiding comprehension of the six concepts in Table 1 about the meaning and practice of democracy. These concepts should be learned in common by all students because they are widely accepted as the distinguishing categories and characteristics by which we judge whether a government is more or less democratic. As students mature, they should encounter and use the same interconnected core concepts in cycles of increasing depth and complexity and in relationship to an ever-broader scope of information.

Mastery of this kind of common knowledge enables citizens to communicate and act together for common civic and political purposes. So common comprehension of core knowledge is the basis for the formation and maintenance of a civic community or democratic civil society. Basic knowledge of democracy, its principles, practices, issues, and history, must be applied effectively to civic and political life if it would be learned thoroughly and used constructively.

Thus, a central facet of education for citizenship in a democracy must be the process by which students develop cognitive civic skills in the second component of Table 2. Cognitive civic skills enable citizens to identify, describe, organise, interpret, explain, compare, and evaluate information and ideas in order to make sense of their political and civic experiences.

Table 2: Components of a global education for democracy

1. Global and international knowledge of democracy (civic knowledge)
    a. Universal concepts and principles on the substance of democracy

b. Perennial issues about the meaning and uses of core ideas

c. Landmark decisions about public policy and constitutional interpretation

d. Constitutions and institutions of representative democratic government

e. Practices of democratic citizenship and the roles of citizens

f. History of democracy in particular states and throughout the world

2. Universal intellectual skills of citizenship in a democracy (cognitive civic skills)

a. Identifying and describing information about political and civic life

b. Analysing and explaining information about political and civic life

c. Synthesising and explaining information about political and civic life

d. Evaluating, taking, and defending positions on public events and issues

e. Thinking critically about conditions of political and civic life

f. Thinking constructively about how to improve political and civic life

g. Thinking comparatively, internationally, and globally about democracy

3. Universal participatory skills of citizenship in a democracy (participatory civic skills)

a. Interacting with other citizens to promote personal and common interests

b. Monitoring public events and issues

c. Deliberating and making decisions about public policy issues

d. Influencing policy decisions on public issues

e. Implementing policy decision on public issues

f. Taking action to improve political and civic life locally, nationally, and globally

4. Universal or global dispositions of citizenship in a democracy (civic dispositions)

a. Affirming the common and equal humanity, dignity, and worth of each person

b. Respecting, protecting, and exercising rights possessed equally by each person

c. Participating responsibly in the political and civic life of the community

d. Practicing self-restraint, personally and institutionally

e. Exemplifying the morality of democratic citizenship

f. Promoting the common good locally, nationally, and globally

---

The third component of Table 2 treats participatory civic skills, which enable citizens to influence public policy decisions and to hold accountable their representatives in government. In combination with cognitive civic skills, participatory civic skills are tools of citizenship whereby individuals, whether acting alone or in groups, can participate effectively to promote personal and common interests in response to public issues.

The fourth and final component of education for citizenship in a democracy pertains to civic dispositions, which are universal traits of character necessary to the preservation and improvement of a constitutional representative democracy. If citizens would enjoy the privileges and rights of their polity, they must take responsibility for them by promoting the common good and participating constructively in the political and civic life of the community. This kind of responsible citizenship depends upon the development and practice of traits such as self-restraint, civility, honesty, trust, courage, compassion, tolerance, temperance, fortitude, respect for the worth and dignity of individuals, and subordination of personal interests to promote the common good.

Effective education for citizenship in a democracy connects the four components in Table 2, which interrelate civic knowledge, cognitive civic skills, participatory civic skills, and civic dispositions. Effective teaching and learning of civic knowledge, for example, requires that it be connected to civic skills and dispositions in various kinds of activities. Elevation of one component over the other—for example, civic knowledge over skills or vice-versa—is a pedagogical flaw that impedes civic learning. Thus, teachers should conjoin core content and processes by which skills and dispositions are developed among students. Core content, however, is the indispensable foundation of an effective education for democracy.

Individuals who have a deep and abiding comprehension of the prevailing principles of democracy, the big ideas that define democratic government and citizenship, are more likely than others to exhibit several desirable dispositions of democratic citizenship, such as a propensity to vote and otherwise participate in political and civic life, political tolerance, political interest, and concern for the common good. Students who comprehend core concepts tend to be more adept in their use of such cognitive skills as organisation and interpretation of information, and they are more likely than others to know and retain information about current political institutions, personalities, and events. Effective teachers of democracy do not stress discrete or unconnected information.

Rather, they focus on integrated ideas of enduring importance; that is, they teach the framework of core concepts that enables the learners to know what democracy is and what it is not, to assess the extent to which their regime and other political systems in the world are more or less democratic, and to think comparatively, internationally, and globally about the various democratic and non democratic systems of the past and present.

Proposition 5: At all levels of preadult education and in programmes of teacher preparation, we should examine the broadly accepted assumptions about the relative worth of democracy in comparison with alternative types of government: In using the six core concepts to comprehend, compare, and evaluate political systems, students should learn that democracy is generally assumed to be the best type of government; but it is not Utopia. It involves neither the pursuit nor promise of perfection. Further, students should recognise the inevitable disparities in every democracy between ideals and realties. These disparities, however, do not invalidate democracy.

Rather, they should challenge students to become citizens committed to reducing the gap between ideals and realities in their polity. Through comparative analysis of political systems of the past and present, students will learn that democracies have tended to be less imperfect than other types of government. Thus, they might conclude that democratic governments are better than non democratic types, because they are the least imperfect. Despite its flaws, democracy in practice has been better than other types of government in protecting human rights, promoting international peace, and fostering economic growth and widespread prosperity. These tangible advantages should be addressed prominently in education for democracy. Thus, students would learn not only what democracy is and how to do it; they would also learn why democracy is good in comparison to alternative types of government.

During the 20 century, values associated with democracy have become accepted universally. Human rights to civil liberty and legal equality are desired by people throughout the world. It seems that people everywhere, if given a choice, will choose democracy and the human rights that a constitutional democracy protects better than alternative forms of government. Freedom in democracy is strongly associated with economic well being. For example, the fully free democracies in the annual Freedom House survey 'account today for $26.8 trillion of the world's annual gross domestic product (GDP), which represents 86 percent of global economic activity.' By contrast, the despotic and autocratic regimes of the world produced in 2002 only '$2.2 trillion in economic output, representing 7 percent of the globe's GDP'.

It seems that the free economic and social systems of a well developed democracy can deliver the goods of wealth and properity. By contrast, the oppressive command economy of a totalitarian system is woefully unproductive. Economic productivity and wealth also seem to be strong indicators of a sustainable democracy. According to a statistical study of democratic countries in the later half of the 20 century, any democracy that had a per capita income of more than $6,000 (in today's dollars) was sustainable. So, economic productivity through a market economy is a key to the durability of a democracy.

The prosperity and freedom in a constitutional democracy seem to encourage international peace. Political scientists and historians have gathered an impressive body of evidence to support the conclusion that 'democracies rarely fight each other'. So a world dominated by democratic and free countries is likely to be a relatively peaceful world. The positive characteristics and consequences of democracy should be a prominent part of a comparative, international, and global education for democracy. And the best case for democracy is made when we teach our students to compare and contrast it with the despotic and totalitarian alternatives to democracy.

Totalitarianism, for example, is the antithesis of constitutional representative democracy. The state and its ruling party command (usually in the name of the people) all aspects of economic, social, and political life. The single party state suppresses alternative sources of power such as civil society organisations and market-based economic activity; it prevents or controls political, social, and economic pluralism; and it controls the media of communication and education. There is a constitution, but there is not constitutionalism in the government, society, and economy.

At its best the totalitarian state provides minimal economic and social security for the masses, but the cost is gross insecurity for the individual's rights to liberty and due process of law. And the productivity of a command economy is deplorable. So, at its best, the totalitarian regime is an undesirable alternative to an authentic constitutional, representative, and free democracy. By teaching the compelling global justifications for democracy, we develop public support needed to sustain it; and the survival of democracy anywhere depends upon wide and deep support among the people. Fortunately, there is ample evidence of strong popular support among most of the world's democracies.

For example, a recently conducted international survey revealed that more than 80% of the people in the fully free democracies express 'support for democracy as an ideal form of government'. In particular, the popular support for democracy in the U.S.A. was 88%, in Estonia 85%, in Latvia 79%, and in Lithuania 86%. Among the democratic countries of Latin America, the mean expression of popular support for the ideals of democracy was 86%. Positive responses among citizens of democratic countries decline sharply, however, when regime performance is judged in terms of the ideals or principles of democracy. For example, only 25%

of citizens in the U.S.A. judged regime performance favourably; in Estonia it was 22%, in Latvia 16%, and in Lithuania 17%. Among the democracies of Latin America, the mean expression of approval for regime performance was 23%.

So, citizens of the world's genuine democracies tend to be highly supportive of what a democracy is supposed to be and greatly disappointed in how it is practiced. The good news in these data is that democracy is clearly and overwhelmingly the preferred political system of the world's diverse peoples. The bad news is the low evaluations of democratic regime performance in terms of the ideals of democracy. Even the bad news, however, has good overtones. Citizens of the world's democracies are ready and willing to think critically about regime performance. This trend can be healthy if it brings about constitutional and institutional reforms to strengthen the best practices of a democratic government.

A properly conceived and conducted 21st-century civic mission in schools can contribute mightily to both the maintenance and improvement of democratic regimes by educating each new generation to understand and use the core concepts by which we define democracy as an ideal type. Thus, citizens would develop competence to think critically in terms of core concepts about the performance of their government, so that the best of it can be retained and the rest of it improved. Finally, through this kind of civic education, students may learn that constitutional representative democracy lives or dies in the minds and hearts of citizens. Its success or failure depends ultimately on the knowledge, skills, habits, and actions of citizens and on the political, social, and economic conditions they create, and not merely on the cleverness or elegance of constitutional design or institutional structures.

6

Civic Education and Democratic Values

Political tolerance, or the willingness to extend procedural liberties such as free speech and association to unpopular or disliked individuals or groups, has long been viewed as essential for a stable and effective democratic system. The extent to which individuals endorse democratic principles such as tolerance figures prominently in debates over the desirability of mass political participation as well, as many scholars argue that increased participation by the "authoritarian-minded" may have deleterious consequences for democratic stability. Thus to assess whether civic education can influence tolerance is to assess its impact on one of the central components of the democratic ethos.

Much research in the new democracies of Eastern Europe, the former Soviet Union, Latin America and South Africa has documented the generally low levels of tolerance and support for minority rights after the emergence of democratic institutions. Though there is also a limited willingness to extend civil liberties to unpopular groups in established democracies, the abysmally low levels of tolerance and support for what Gibson and Duch term "minoritarian" principles in developing contexts may pose a significant danger to the future stability of these democratic systems. Indeed, Gibson's finding that individuals who embraced democratic principles were more likely to resist the attempted coup staged in Moscow in 1991 suggests that increasing tolerance can be instrumental in the consolidation of fledgling democratic regimes.

Given the powerful racial, ethnic and political animosities that characterise many developing democracies, as well as the strains placed on these systems by poor economic and political performance, it is difficult to imagine a more pressing task for civic education in these settings than to raise support for the exercise of democratic political liberties and "the rules of the democratic game." Aside from these practical concerns, examining the effect of civic education on tolerance has several more general theoretical aims.

First, the results can shed light on the extent to which democratic political orientations can be affected at all by short-term stimuli, as opposed to changing more slowly due to long-term economic modernisation, generational change, the ability of political parties and elites to manage social conflict and the gradual diffusion of democratic ideals through the international mass media. A growing body of literature suggests that support for democracy and democratic values may be susceptible to influence from short-term economic, political, and experiential factors. A finding that civic education influences tolerance — an orientation that has been thought by many to be difficult to change — would lend significant support to the view that political culture in general is susceptible to short-term influence. And such changes may then at least partially be within the reach of active efforts at manipulation by governments, political elites, or international actors.

Second, the exploration of civic education's effects on tolerance in developing democracies affords an important real-world test of recent experimental findings that individual levels of tolerance may change considerably in response to argumentation and efforts at political persuasion. As opposed to the notion that individuals have fixed, long-standing attitudes toward tolerance, this line of research views tolerance as the product of judgments made by individuals, depending on the considerations they bring to bear at the time, their prior store of political information, attachment to democratic norms, and psychological openness to change.

Civic education programmes are institutionalised attempts at attitude change. They aim to change tolerance judgments by imparting new information to individuals, information that promotes the linkage of tolerance to more abstract democratic values, to prior political and psychological dispositions, and to more general positive outcomes associated with democratic systems. Hence an examination of the effects of civic education can provide more theoretical insights into how values may change in response to efforts at persuasion outside the laboratory setting, and increase our understanding of the conditions under which value change is likely to occur.

Development of Political Tolerance

For the past several decades, the United States and many West European countries have devoted considerable resources to providing democracy assistance and strengthening civil society in emerging democracies around the world. As Quigley notes, there are now a "plethora of public and private international actors involved in these efforts .... [including]...most multilateral organisations, regional development banks, major bilateral assistance programmes, as well as literally thousands of non-governmental organisations." Some of these activities centre around the training of lawyers, journalists and other social elites in the rule of law, in assisting constitutional reform, and in strengthening democratic political parties, non-governmental organisations, and other elements of a country's newly-emerging civil society.

Some of the activities, though, are directed explicitly at promoting support for democratic norms and values among ordinary citizens. These efforts constitute "civic education programmes," and range from the adoption of new curricula in primary and secondary schools to teach young people about democracy, to programmes that provide instruction about the social and political rights of women, to voter education programmes, to neighbourhood problem-solving programmes that bring individuals in contact with local authorities for purposes of promoting collective action to benefit local communities. How much impact on a value such as political tolerance are civic education programmes likely to have?

From the traditional perspective of political culture and socialisation, the answer would appear to be very little. According to this view, change in a country's democratic political culture should occur very slowly, primarily in response to structural factors such as economic modernisation, generational replacement, or the long-term experience of citizens with rotations of power and a responsible opposition structure among the country's political parties. The glacial change in cultural values assumed in this view was echoed in much of the early literature in political socialisation, which argued that orientations learned early in life "structured" later adult attitudes and limited the extent to which basic values and preferences would change in response to short-term stimuli. The voluminous literature on the specific determinants of political tolerance offers much support for this view.

Many of the most important predictors of tolerance would appear to be well beyond the ability and scope of even the most intensive short-term civic education programme. For example, individuals who are more dogmatic, mistrustful, inflexible and "psychologically insecure" are less willing to extend procedural liberties to individuals or groups with who they disagree, and these kinds of deeply-rooted personality characteristics are likely to be relatively impervious to change. Similarly, political and religious conservatism have also been linked consistently to levels of political tolerance, as have attitudes towards out-groups and the potential threats that they may represent.

Only for attitudes about groups and threat perceptions would civic education appear to have a chance for success, but, as Sullivan and Transue note, threat perceptions contain a large "chronic, dispositional role" as well. And attitudes about racial outgroups, for example those forged in contemporary South Africa, are likely to be deeply rooted in the experiences of living under the apartheid regime, making it difficult to undo a lifetime of socialisation in a series of democracy workshops. Recent developments in the literature, however, suggest that democratic values, and political tolerance in particular, may be more malleable than previously thought.

First, a steady stream of findings over the past several decades has shown that more immediate variables such as the individual's perceptions of current economic conditions, assessments of governmental competence, and political and social participation can affect orientations such as the individual's "normative commitment to democracy," and the internalisation of democratic values, social and institutional trust, and political efficacy. The widespread demonstration of such effects has led many to conclude that, although early socialisation and social structural factors play a role in determining democratic attitudes, these factors must be augmented by variables related to adult political experiences. Mishler and Rose, for example, explicitly posit what they call a "lifetime learning model," where attitudes learned early in life are continuously updated as these "early attitudes and beliefs are reinforced or challenged by subsequent experiences." Clearly, such a view allows a greater potential influence of civic education as another short-term experiential effect on the individual's level of political tolerance.

Second, a related stream of recent research has challenged the notion that tolerance is a stable or fixed individual-level attitude, arguing instead that individual judgments are highly responsive to political argumentation and efforts at persuasion. Using a variety of innovative experimental and quasi-experimental research designs, these studies have shown that tolerance can be quite pliable, changing in predictable ways according to the nature of the information presented to respondents. Kuklinski et al, for example, showed that tolerance responses could differ substantially, depending on whether respondents were encouraged to view a situation through an "emotional" or "cognitive" frame.

Similarly, Nelson et al. showed that experimentally emphasising the frame of "rights of free speech" or the "need for public order" in a given tolerance situation had a significant effect on whether individuals' attitudes on those dimensions would be brought to bear in formulating their responses. And Gibson, Marcus et al. 1995, and

Sniderman et al. have used the "counterargument technique" to great effect, showing that tolerance changes considerably after respondents are presented with reasons why they might reconsider their initial view. This work has called into question much of the received wisdom in the field; most importantly, it has shown that, at least in the laboratory or in experimental survey situations, substantial change in tolerance through political persuasion is possible.

The recent linkage of the tolerance literature to persuasion and attitude change research is an important one, and one with clear implications for the analysis of the impact of civic education. Civic education is properly viewed as an institutionalised mechanism for attempted attitude and value change in newly democratising societies. Through means of workshops, community problem-solving activities, voter education drives, and the like, it is hoped that individuals will be persuaded by the messages conveyed to convert towards tolerance and towards the internalisation of other democratic orientations. As such, it may be expected that the conditions that facilitate attitude change in general should facilitate attitude change via the mechanism of civic education.

The vast literature on attitude change in psychology and political psychology contains a number of theories specifying alternative routes to persuasion. There is, however, unanimity on one fundamental point with direct relevance for the analysis here: attitude change does not occur uniformly across populations upon exposure to persuasive messages. That is, we should expect to see conditional effects of exposure to messages on the likelihood of change, as certain kinds of messages are more likely to bring about change, and certain kinds of individuals are more receptive to change than others.

For example, McGuire's well-known "reception-acceptance" model of attitude change, adapted and extended into political psychology by Zaller, asserts that the reception of messages varies directly with the individual's level of interest, motivation, and political awareness, while the individual's acceptance of messages varies inversely with those same variables, as highly aware individuals are less likely to accept messages that run counter to their prior attitudes and predispositions. Thus attitude change is most likely to occur among individuals who are moderately aware and interest: less interested and aware individuals are unlikely to receive messages and more engaged individuals are unlikely to accept them.

Other models of attitude change stress the characteristics of the message, the degree of trust placed in the source of the message, the intensity of the previously-held attitude, the degree to which the attitude is embedded in a more complex associative network, and many others. All of these variables operate as mediating factors, establishing firmly the observation that attitude change occurs only under certain conditions for certain kinds of individuals. What factors are likely to condition whether individuals receive and accept tolerance messages in the real-world context of civic education? These are: factors related to the nature of the civic education experience itself, factors related to the individual's store of political information and general levels of awareness, and factors related to the individual's prior attitudes and values.

Attitude change depends first on the individual's reception of a particular message. In the civic education context, the reception of a tolerance message should depend on the individual's frequency of attending civic education sessions. More importantly, tolerance messages are difficult ones to accept in general. The notion that individuals ought to extend civil liberties to hated and potentially dangerous groups is not only "unnatural" in many ways, but also rooted in fairly abstract conceptions about due process, democratic procedures, reciprocity and political competition.

Thus frequent exposures may be needed before tolerance messages begin to be understood. If this is the case, then there may not be monotonic increases in political tolerance as individuals attend more civic education sessions; rather there may be threshold effects, such that no change is observed until individuals are exposed repeatedly to protolerance messages. The type of instruction the individual receives in civic education is likely to matter as well. Much research in social psychology suggests that a significant source of attitude change is role-playing behaviour, as individuals come to adopt attitudes and cognitions that are consistent with the behaviours that they are acting out.

It may be expected, therefore, that civic education programmes that make use of more active methodologies to instruct participants – role playing, dramatisations, group decision-making, and the like, to have a greater effect on individual orientations than lecture-based instruction. We also expect a series of conditional relationships between civic education, tolerance and certain attitudes and attributes of the individual. Following Zaller, civic education messages will be accepted to the extent that the individual's psychological and political dispositions are otherwise favourable towards tolerance, and the individual is able to make linkages between the messages received in civic education and those prior dispositions.

That is, individuals who are able to "contextualise" or integrate the tolerance messages into a supportive system of democratic orientations are more likely to change than individuals whose prior attitudes and values are either anti-democratic or too compartmentalised to allow links from a persuasive message to other pro-democracy attitudes and values. This suggests that the individual's prior political awareness and motivation should be critical in the attitude change process, as should the extent to which the individuals prior orientations are more or less favourable towards democracy in general.

Political information and interest are likely to be important conditioning variables in attitude change for several reasons.

First, these factors make it more likely that individuals will receive messages from civic education, as more interested and informed individuals may be likely to attend civic education in the first place, and continue to attend after an initial experience.

Second, politically aware and knowledgeable individuals will likely have the cognitive skills to understand the message from civic education to which they are exposed; even repeated exposures for individuals who lack the cognitive abilities to process them may not be enough to bring about attitude change.

And third, politically aware individuals are best equipped to make the necessary associations between the tolerance messages and other supportive values. That is, higher levels of information and interest are likely to lead to greater contextualisation of civic education messages, and hence greater acceptance, when individuals' other attitudes incline them to be more tolerant. However, awareness and interest may have curvilinear effects on the likelihood of attitude change. At the highest levels of awareness, individuals who are predisposed to be democratic may already be relatively tolerant, and individuals who are predisposed against tolerance should possess enough countervailing information to resist the new information. Thus we may expect change to be concentrated among individuals with enough prior information and cognitive skills to receive and comprehend tolerance messages, but not enough countervailing information to resist them.

Finally, several attitudes, perceptions, and values should predispose individuals to either accept or reject the tolerance messages in civic education.

First, as the discussion thus far has made clear, the individual's prior adherence to other democratic values represents important predispositions to change. If individuals are more democratic in their orientations to begin with — that is, accept principles such as the rule of law, the need for political liberty over social order, and believe that individuals can influence the political process — then they should be less likely to resist tolerance messages, and more able to see the connections between those messages and their other supportive democratic beliefs.

Second, personality factors such as dogmatism or close-mindedness were found by Gibson to impede efforts at persuasion. In Zaller's terms, dogmatic individuals will be more likely to resist messages that promote tolerance; their inflexible belief system is unlikely to change generally, and also unlikely to change towards a value to which they are predisposed to oppose in the first place.

Further, it may be hypothesised that perceptions related to the immediate political and economic situation of the country will join longer standing predispositions to affect the likelihood of accepting tolerance messages. In situations where individuals have little other experience with democratic institutions and governance, the associations that are made with tolerance messages are likely to be based on individuals' overall satisfaction with the economic and political performance of the democratic system itself.

Hence when messages promoting the applied democratic value of tolerance are received, individuals may naturally be more likely to accept or reject those messages based on other associations they currently have with the political system. In the absence of long-standing experiences with democracy, performance ratings are all that many individuals have - especially those with lower levels of prior political information. For this reason perceptions about the system's economic and political performance may represent a powerful conditioning factor that determines the individual's susceptibility to persuasive messages via civic education.

Civic Education Research Programmes

Dominican Republic

The first of the programmes studied was conducted by a national elections oriented nongovernmental organisation, Participación Ciudadana (PC). For the 1996 presidential elections, PC created another group, called La Red de los Observadores Electorales, to organise and train youth and adults to serve as election observers in 1996 and to conduct a quick count of the vote. The programme ran from 1995 to mid-1996, although PC activities continued into 1997, still focused on elections.

Of those in the sample 14% of the respondents were exposed to PC and Red training sessions but did not eventually work as election observers. The second programme was conducted by a newly formed nongovernmental organisation, Grupo Accion por la Democracia (GAD). The programme was conducted in two phases, with the first phase dedicated to a general educational programme concerning basic political rights and obligations in a democracy, primarily through a lecture format.

The second phase brought these people together to hold a series of national and local issues fora to discuss problems and solutions in specific policy areas, such as justice, health, and education. Local government authorities attended these fora as well. The two phases were intended to create a national NGO with a network of local branches outside of Santo Domingo and to mobilise citizens to participate in these new structures. The programme ran from November 1995 to October 1996.

The third programme was part of a larger community finance and small business development programme for women conducted through women's small business NGO, Asociación Dominicana para el Desarrollo de la Mujer (ADOPEM). The programme trained women community leaders in women's rights, democratic values, democracy in the family, and self-esteem, using a classroom/workshop format, and ran from January 1996 to January 1997.

The fourth programme studied was conducted by a local NGO affiliated with a local radio station in La Vega, Radio Santa María (RSM). The project trained intermediaries (typically leaders of rural towns) who then conducted civic education in their local communities. The subject matter focused on civic knowledge and values, such as rights and duties in a democracy, the importance of participation, and democracy in the family. RSM ran two consecutive projects, from 1994 to 1995 and from 1995 to December 1996. In all of the programmes in the Dominican Republic except Radio

Santa Maria, treatment samples were drawn from lists of participants provided by the implementing organisations.

For the Radio Santa Maria programme, only lists of the "leaders" or first-stage participants were maintained, and we obtained names of ordinary participants through "snowball" sampling methods from interviewers with the first stage participants. The number of individuals interviewed from the four programmes totalled 1018. The strategy for obtaining appropriate control samples was to select non-participants at random in each of the regions where the programmes were conducted.

The sampling began with a national stratified random sample of 50 municipalities, as the PC programme operated nationwide, and GAD operated in all areas except for Santo Domingo, the country's capital. Individuals were selected for inclusion in the sample in proportion to the population of the selected municipality. This control sample was then supplemented with an oversample of individuals in La Vega, where the Radio Santa Maria programme operated, and an oversample of women in the four areas where ADOPEM conducted its training. The number of individuals interviewed for the control groups was 1017.

The in-country survey was conducted by the Instituto de Estudios de Población y Desarrollo (IEPD), the statistical office affiliated with PROFAMILIA. Data were collected from February to April 1998. The response rate for the survey was an excellent 90.5%, with 98% response for the participant sample and 83.7% response for the control group. Due to the lack of appropriate Census-type data, it is impossible to assess definitively the representativeness of the sample, but the age, educational level, and marital status of our control sample closely resemble the levels seen in the 1993 DEMOS survey conducted on behalf of USAID, which at the time represented the last official survey of political values of the Dominican Republic population before the current study.

South Africa

The South African study included three programmes that conducted civic education among black and coloured adults. The first was run by the National Institute for Public Interest Law and Research (NIPILAR). NIPILAR is "the lead organisation of a Consortium operating at the national level in the field of public interest law, rights education with emphasis on women and children's rights, as well as the Constitution and Bill of Rights education. The activities aim to promote the

1) respect, practice and fulfillment of human, legal, and civil rights;
2) respect for the rights of women and children and
3) a widespread awareness of human rights and democracy".

One of the main civic education programmes conducted by NIPILAR over the past several years was its Women's Rights programme, designed to promote awareness of the United Nations Women and Children's Rights Convention.

The second programme was operated through the Community Law Centre-Durban (CLC). CLC is part of the Consortium described above, and thus has many of the same goals and activities as NIPILAR. CLC, however, operates almost exclusively within the province of KwaZulu Natal, where NIPILAR does not operate. Its primary activities are to coordinate approximately 30 rural legal advice offices in the province. The advice offices provide assistance to community members on legal and human rights issues. Democracy and civic education workshops are also conducted through the advice centres.

The third South Africa programme was conducted by Lawyers for Human Rights (LHR). LHR is a national organisation aiming to increase the awareness of human and democratic rights in South Africa. The organisation holds an extensive series of workshops yearly on democracy and human rights issues, with different aspects of democracy receiving particular emphasis in different years. Workshops in the last two years have emphasised the Constitution and the Bill of Rights, and participation in politics, respectively.

The first two groups were selected primarily because of the support that USAID-South Africa has provided for their civic education efforts. LHR was included in the study in order to examine a non-USAID-funded group, and because it is a well-known NGO promoting democracy and human rights in South Africa. LHR also conducted civic education in eight of the nine provinces of South Africa; NIPILAR was also more or less national in focus, while CLC-Durban's area of operation was mainly within one province, KwaZulu Natal.

The three NGOS operate in generally similar fashion with regard to their civic education activities. Representatives from the central offices train a core group of individuals, called "paralegals," in democracy and human rights instruction. These activities, generally known as Training of Trainers (ToT), consume a considerable amount of the group's time and resources. The paralegals then go on to operate offices in villages and towns across country, from which they provide a number of services for individual residents. Some of these services have nothing to do with civic education, for example providing advice on economic development or labour law.

However, the paralegals are also expected to conduct community workshops on different aspects of democratic governance and human rights. As in the Dominican Republic, the treatment group interviews were obtained through sampling lists of civic education participants provided by the three NGOs (either national representatives or the facilitators or paralegals who ran the civic education programmes in each of the areas).

Participants were selected systematically from the lists whenever addresses and contact information was provided. In regions where no lists of names and addresses existed, the facilitators or paralegals themselves located the requisite number of participants and provided contact information to the South African survey organisation, Markinor, which collected the data. The control group of non-participants in South Africa was designed slightly differently than in the Dominican Republic. Instead of aiming to produce a random sample of the South African black or coloured population, the researchers attempted to introduce more rigorous experimental control at the outset by "mirroring" the participant sample on a number of important demographic dimensions.

Interviewers were instructed to conduct an interview with a civic education participant selected according to the procedures just described, and then to conduct an identical interview in the same area with a person who had not participated in civic education. The control group respondent was to be the same race, gender, age group, and educational stratum as the participant. Interviewers were instructed to make a systematic selection of houses, beginning with the third house from the civic education participant who had been interviewed, in order to find an appropriate non-participant for inclusion.

These sampling procedures produced a total of 1550 interviews for the study, with the final data collection conducted between 10 May and 1 June 1999. The questionnaires were translated into Zulu, Xhosa, Tswana, Northern Sotho, Southern Sotho, and Afrikaans so that respondents could be interviewed in the language with which they felt most comfortable. The final sample consisted of: 475 adult participants in civic education, and 475 adult non-participants who were matched on race, gender, age and education with the participant group. 10 individuals from the treatment group were eliminated from the analysis because it became unclear in the course of the interview how many workshops they had attended, or whether they had been exposed to civic education "treatment" at all.

Bivariate Findings

The first step in examining civic education's propensity to inspire more tolerant attitudes in the Dominican Republic and South Africa is simply to compare the responses for civic education participants with the control group in both countries. Table 1 displays the simple percentage differences in tolerant responses between individuals who were exposed to varying amount of civic education: the percentages for individuals who received no civic education are displayed in the first column of results, followed by the percentages for individuals who attended only one or two civic education sessions, and then percentages for those who attended civic education more frequently. A "tolerant" response was indicated when individuals "strongly agreed" or "agreed" that an atheist, militarist, communist, racist or sexist should be allowed to speak in public or organise peaceful demonstrations.

Table 1: Tolerance by Frequency of Civic Education Dominican Republic and South Africa

	Control Group	*Civic Education 1-2x*	*Civic Education 3x or more*	*Strength of Association*
Dominican Republic				
Would allow an atheist to. . .				
Speak in Public	42.9	46.5	52.4	.14**
Vote	52.4	61.5	62.7	.17**
Organise a Peaceful Demonstration	52.5	52.7	60.0	.10**
Would allow a militarist to. . .				
Speak in Public	39.3	37.6	43.4	.05
Vote	41.0	44.8	46.5	.09*
Organise Peaceful Demonstration	48.6	47.0	54.5	.08*
Would allow a communist to. . .				
Speak in Public	51.0	52.7	68.9	.28**
Vote	58.5	59.7	75.0	.24**
Organise Peaceful Demonstration	54.9	58.6	68.4	.28**
Tolerance Scale Score	2.43	2.50	2.70	.16**
Number of Cases	1019	407	611	
South Africa				
Would allow an atheist to. . .				
Speak in Public	38.0	37.7	45.3	.04*
Organise Peaceful Demonstration	43.9	42.2	52.0	.05*
Would allow a racist to. . .				
Speak in Public	32.7	38.8	47.4	.18**
Organise Peaceful Demonstration	41.9	40.3	50.8	.06**
Would allow a sexist to. . .				
Speak in Public	41.1	37.7	44.5	.00
Organise Peaceful Demonstration	39.6	40.3	52.0	.11**
Tolerance Scale Score	2.28	2.29	2.50	.09**
Number of Cases	475	331	134	

$^{**}p<.05$ $^{*}p<.10$

As can be seen in the top half of Table 1, the raw differences between tolerant responses for the three civic education groups are moderate in magnitude in the Dominican Republic. Differences of approximately 10 percentage points exist between the tolerant responses of the control group and those with the highest frequency of exposure to civic education. The largest differences are provoked by questions related to communists (14-18 percentage points), with smaller differences on responses towards atheists (8-10 points) and militarists (4-7 points). The gamma statistic in the last column confirms that there is a relatively large association between civic education exposure and tolerance toward communists, with associations of smaller magnitude between civic education and tolerance towards militarists and atheists.

Individuals in the frequent civic education group are significantly more tolerant on the overall scale than individuals in the control group (2.70 versus 2.43), with a corresponding Eta value of .16. The bottom half of the table shows that civic education significantly influences tolerance in South Africa as well, though the patterns are less pronounced than in the Dominican Republic. The differences between the control group and those exposed frequently to civic education varies from 4 percentage points (allowing a sexist to speak) to 14 percentage points (allowing a racist to speak), with the overall average difference being about 9 points.

There are few remarkable differences in the tolerance according atheists as opposed to racists or sexists, nor does tolerance depend on whether the question concerns speaking in public or organising peaceful demonstrations. The gammas in South Africa, ranging from zero to .18, confirm the slightly smaller differences between the civic education groups than in the Dominican Republic.

Interestingly, the results from both countries show that there is very little difference in the tolerant responses between individuals in the control group and individuals who attended only one of two civic education workshops.

That is, differences in tolerance emerge only between the control group and individuals who attended three or more civic education sessions. This pattern is confirmed through further analysis, as simple *t*-tests between the control group and the infrequent civic education group shows few significant differences. This provides initial support for the hypothesis earlier that there may be threshold effects for civic education on political tolerance: attending one or two workshops may simply not be enough to effect value change, and repeated exposures to democratic civic instruction may be necessary for any effect whatsoever to occur. The threshold pattern seen for the Dominican Republic, whereby infrequent exposure to civic education has little effect on tolerance responses, is even more pronounced in South Africa.

On most items, there is absolutely no difference between the control group and those who attended only one or two civic education workshops. This pattern was confirmed in further analyses: simple t-tests of the differences between the control group and all civic education recipients in South Africa shows no statistically significant results, and the simple correlations between the number of workshops the individual attended and tolerant responses similarly showed few significant relationships. Similarly, the overall tolerance scale mean is nearly identical for the control group (2.28) and the infrequent exposure group (2.29); this figure rises to 2.50 for those in the highest exposure group. Thus there is strong preliminary support for the notion that civic education can have some effect on tolerance in both the Dominican Republic and South Africa, but that effects are seen only after individuals are exposed repeatedly to democratic messages.

It is important to emphasise that the results in Table 1 represent only the raw, or unadjusted, differences between tolerant responses of the control and the two civic education groups. That is, they do not take into account any of the possible selection biases related to civic education exposure. It is likely that certain kinds of individuals are more likely to receive civic education training than others, for example, individuals who are more politically interested or more highly educated, or who belong to voluntary organisations. It is essential to bring variables reflecting these background factors directly into the analysis to assess more accurately the impact of civic education on political tolerance.

Tables 2 and 3 present the results of multivariate analysis of the effects of political tolerance in the Dominican Republic and South Africa, respectively. In order to allow for the possibility of threshold effects, as suggested in Table 1, two dummy variables were constructed to signify whether the respondent had attended one or two civic education workshops, or whether the respondent had attended three or more sessions. In model (1) in both tables, the effects of the civic education dummies are shown, controlling for a series of demographic, psychological, and political variables that may relate to both political tolerance and to the likelihood of exposure to civic education.

In model (2) in the tables, additional variables related to democratic values, civic competence, and performance evaluations are included in both countries. The two models distinguish background factors from democratic orientations and performance evaluations that are more likely to be affected by civic education programmes. Thus comparing model (2) to model (1) provides a means for assessing the extent to which civic education affects political tolerance directly, as well as indirectly through its potential effects on other values and orientations. The results of these analyses indicate that civic education has significant direct effects on political tolerance in both countries, even after observed variables are introduced as controls to take potential selection biases into account.

But as in Table 1, these effects exist only when individuals are exposed to three or more civic education sessions. In model (1) in Table 1, it can be seen individuals who were exposed to only one or two sessions in the Dominican Republic were no more likely to report tolerant responses than the control group, once other variables in the model are taken into account. By contrast, individuals who attended three or more sessions were, on average, .12 units higher on the tolerance scale than individuals who received no civic education. The effect of civic education on tolerance can also be expressed in terms of what is known in experimental or quasi-experimental research as the "effect coefficient" or "Cohen's *d*".

In the multiple regression context, *d* is equal to the unstandardised regression coefficient divided by the standard error of estimate, which conveys a sense of how much of an effect a treatment has in standard deviation terms on the dependent variable, once the effects of all other control variables are taken into account. Thus the .12 coefficient for the effect of civic education indicates that a three or more session "treatment" of civic education in the Dominican Republic is associated with a .12 standard deviation increase in tolerance. Model (1) also shows that a substantial amount of the differences in tolerance between civic education groups observed in Table 1 was attributable to background characteristics of civic education participants rather than the programmes themselves.

Frequent civic education recipients were likely to have characteristics associated with higher tolerance to begin with. That is, civic education recipients were more likely to be more highly educated, younger, more open to compromise, less right wing, less likely to attend regular religious services, and more attentive to the media than were individuals in the control group. As expected, many of these variables were related to tolerance as well, and these spurious effects accounted for nearly half of the original observed differences between the treatment and control groups.

Yet even after these factors were controlled, exposure to civic education still has a significant impact on tolerance, and the effect coefficient of .12 (and the standardised coefficient of .07) ranks it at approximately the same magnitude of importance as urban compared to rural residence, or moving from centre-left to right wing in political ideology. This is evidence of a relatively small but substantively meaningful effect of civics instruction on Dominicans' level of political tolerance.

Model (1) in Table 3 shows the analogous analysis conducted for the South African sample. The overall explanatory power of the model is lower than in the Dominican Republic; among the control variables, only education, age, race and the individual's openness to other cultures are significant predictors of tolerance. Yet controlling for these factors, the effect of civic education remains significant, and follows the same threshold pattern seen in model (1) in the Dominican Republic. There are no differences on tolerance between the control group and individuals who attended only one or two workshops, whereas individuals who were exposed to civics workshops more frequently showed significant increases in tolerance over the control group.

The average tolerance score for individuals who attended three or more workshops was .20 units higher than the score for individuals in the control group, controlling for all other variables in the model. This translates into an effect coefficient of .24, meaning that a three workshop "treatment" of civic education is associated with a nearly one-quarter (adjusted) standard deviation change in political tolerance. This is an even larger net effect than seen in the Dominican Republic, and one of the largest effects in the South African model overall. Interestingly, the demographic and political differences between the control group and individuals who attended civic education sessions in South Africa was not nearly as great as that seen in the Dominican Republic.

Individuals who attended civic education workshops were only somewhat more highly educated, more politically interested, more active in secondary groups, and more attentive to the media than were individuals in the control group, and (by design) the groups were identical in terms of age, gender, race, and place of residence. And most of these variables were themselves only marginally related to tolerance. Thus the confounding effects of selection bias were more limited in South Africa, and for this reason the magnitude of the effects of civic education in Table 1 and in Table 3 is nearly identical.

Model (2) in Tables 2 and 3 includes additional control variables related to more general democratic values, civic competence, and performance evaluations. Previous research has found a substantial constraining function of more general democratic values on tolerance, such that support for more abstract democratic principles such as the value of liberty over social order, or support for the rule of law is more likely to lead to specific applications of political tolerance. Similarly, there is also some evidence that individuals who are more efficacious and knowledgeable about politics may be more willing to extend procedural liberties to unpopular groups, and to the extent that civic education increases these attributes of civic competence, tolerance may increase as well.

Finally, in line with the "lifetime learning model," much recent research has shown that perceptions of economic and political performance are related to increases in democratic orientations. Although civic education is not necessarily designed to influence these kinds of orientations, it may nevertheless be the case that exposure to civics instruction heightens individuals' attention to the current performance of the economy and incumbent authorities. If these variables themselves are then related to tolerance, this would represent an important indirect route for civic education to effect attitude change. The results show that the direct effects of civic education on tolerance far outweigh its indirect influences.

In Table 2, it can be seen that the unstandardised effect of attending three or more civic education sessions drops only slightly from .12 to .10. Among the variables added to the model, only political efficacy influences the level of Dominicans' tolerance, while support for liberty, political knowledge, and concern about the national economy are irrelevant predictors. This indicates that the indirect effects of civic education through efficacy, knowledge and values and economic orientations are slight.

The same pattern of results is found in South Africa, as is shown in model (2) of Table 3. The effect of attending three or more civic education workshops falls to .17, compared to its value of .20 in model (1), about a 15% drop once the democratic values, competence measures, and performance evaluations are taken into account. Only two of the measured intervening variables, however, themselves have significant effects on tolerance, thus limiting the potential for the indirect influences of civic education.

Table 2: The Effect of Civic Education on Political Tolerance, Dominican Republic

	Model 1		*Model 2*	
	B	*beta*	*B*	*beta*
Frequency of Civic Education				
One or Two Sessions	.04	.02	.02	.01
Three or More Sessions	.12**	.07	.10**	.06
Democratic Values and Civic Competence				
Support for Liberty			-.02	-.02
Political Efficacy			.12**	.12
Political Knowledge			.02	.04
Economic Evaluations				
Unemployment, Inflation concerns low			-.02	-.01
Psychological Predispositions				
Open to Compromise	.14**	.13	.14**	.13
Low Paternalism	.06**	.05	.05*	.04
Demographic and Political Controls				
Age	.12*	.17	.09	.14
Age Squared	-.02*	-.16	-.01	-.12
Black Respondent	.06	.03	.06	.03
White Respondent	.08	.03	.08	.03
Gender (1=Male)	-.01 -	.01	-.04	-.03
Education	.09**	.20	.07**	.17
Income	.01	.02	.01	.01
Church Attendance	-.02**	-.04	-.02*	-.04
Santo Domingo Resident	.14**	.07	.13**	.07
Other Urban District	.09**	.06	.09**	.06
Group Memberships	.07	.01	.04	.01
Political Ideology (Right-Wing)	-.04**	-.06	-.04**	-.06

Political Interest	.01	.00	-.03	-.03
Media Use	.08**	.10	.06**	.08
Constant	1.52		1.46	
R-Squared	.17		.18	
Standard Error of Estimate	.69		.69	
N=2037 (both Models)				

*p<.10 **p<.05

Individuals who support the more abstract value of liberty in South Africa are more likely to endorse specific applications of tolerance, and individuals who are more politically knowledgeable are more tolerant as well; neither efficacy nor any of performance evaluations show significant effects. Thus the direct effect of civics instruction is by far the more important influence of civic education on political tolerance in both the Dominican Republic and South Africa.

Table 3: The Effect of Civic Education on Political Tolerance, South Africa

	Model 1		*Model 2*	
	B	*beta*	*B*	*beta*
Frequency of Civic Education				
One or Two Workshops	.04	.01	.03	.02
Three or More Workshops	.20**	.08	.17**	.07
Democratic Values and Civic Competence				
Support for Liberty			.09**	.10
Political Efficacy			.06	.05
Political Knowledge			.07**	.09
Economic and Political Evaluations				
Perceived Government Performance			-.06	-.05
Perceived Personal Economic Situation			-.01	-.01
Perceived National Economic Situation			-.04	-.06
Psychological Predispositions				
Open to Other Cultures	.11*	.07	.11**	.06

Positive Affect towards Racial Out-groups	.02	.01	.01	.01
Demographic and Political Controls				
Age	.25*	.33	.20**	.26
Age Squared	-.04*	-.29	-.03	-.23
Race (1=Coloured)	.48**	.17	.46**	.17
Gender (1=Male)	.06	.03	.02	.01
Education	.05*	.08	.03	.05
Income	.01	.00	-.01	-.01
Church Attendance	-.01	-.00	.01	.01
City Resident	.05	.03	.04	.02
Group Memberships	-.15	-.04	-.21*	-.06
Political Interest	-.04	-.03	-.05	-.04
Media Use	.05	.05	.04	.04
Constant	1.87		2.02	
R-Squared	.06		.08	
Standard Error of Estimate	.83		.82	
N=940 (both Models)				

*p<.10 **p<.05

Role of Pedagogical Methods

Persuasion is most likely to occur under certain conditions related to the nature of the individual's exposure to pro-tolerance messages, and conditions related to attitudes and prior attitudes of the individual. The results thus far reinforce the conditional relationship between civic education and political tolerance. Civic education's influence on tolerance depends on the frequency of exposure to tolerance messages; three or more sessions are necessary for any effect of civic education to occur.

To measure the extent of exposure to participatory methods, respondents were asked which of the following methods were used in the programmes they attended (breaking into small groups, staging plays or dramatisations, playing games, problem-solving, and simulations or role-playing). In the Dominican Republic respondents were asked further whether respondents had much opportunity to express their own views in the programme, and in South Africa whether workshops had included "staging mock trials of legal proceedings," or "staging mock elections or other kinds of political activities." There was a moderate amount of collinearity between the frequency of civic education exposure and exposure to participatory teaching methodologies, making it difficult to isolate the effect of each variable.

The results strongly support the hypothesis that participatory teaching methods are more effective at influencing tolerance in South Africa, with a more equivocal finding in the Dominican Republic. Analysis including the "participatory methods" dummy variable showed that, in South Africa, both frequency of exposure to civic education and the participatory methods used in the instruction have significant effects on levels of political tolerance. Individuals with frequent exposures to civic education, and exposure to participatory teaching methodologies, increased their tolerance score by .25 over the control group, compared to the value of .17 when considering exposure to civic education alone.

In the Dominican Republic, the combination of frequent exposures and active methodologies led to a .14 increase in tolerance, compared to the value of .10 for three or more exposures alone. Thus, the more participatory methods used in instruction, the greater the change in political tolerance in both countries. The magnitude of these changes, however, is not all that substantial beyond the effects of repeated civic education exposures, especially in the Dominican Republic.

7

Deliberative Democracy

Democratic theorists invoke different conceptions of democracy. Associations or committees may seek to resolve internal disagreements by implementing democratic decision-making procedures. This usually entails deciding the issue by a show of hands and being bound by the majority decision. When applied to a political association this popular understanding of democracy requires that all citizens be entitled to an equal vote and that the will of the majority rules. But the shortcomings of this simple characterisation of democracy are easily illustrated. For example, if all citizens have an equal vote but only have the option of voting for one political party we would not want to say that such an arrangement fulfilled the requirements of a true democracy.

Political equality, which underlies our commitment to democracy, is not secured by simply ensuring each person is entitled to an equal vote and that the will of the majority rules. Robert Dahl provides the following comprehensive list of opportunities that must be satisfied if a decision-making process is to be called "democratic".

1. Effective participation.
2. Equality in voting.

3. Gaining enlightened understanding.
4. Exercising final control over the agenda.
5. Inclusion of adults.

Utilising Dahl's criteria of democracy will provide us with a useful introduction to the themes of deliberative democracy. For Dahl, 'the policies of an association must always be open to change by the members of the association, if they so choose'. Dahl's concern is that a minority interest might be allowed to decide the political agenda if we do not ensure that the constitutional arrangements satisfy this fourth criterion. If a minority interest has control of the agenda then the association cannot be characterised as an association of political equals. This fourth criterion is the subject of much debate between procedural and constitutional democrats. The latter will be reluctant to place complete control over the political agenda in the hands of the demos for fears that unjust outcomes might occur.

Aggregative Model of Democracy

According to this model of democracy, decision-making processes ought simply to aggregate the preferences of citizens in choosing public officials and parties. An outcome is thus just, according to this account of democracy, if it mirrors the preferences of the majority of people. This is what is known as the aggregative model of democracy. Individuals in the polity have varying preferences about what they want government institutions to do. They know that other individuals also have preferences, which may or may not match their own.

Democracy is a competitive process in which political parties and candidates offer their platforms and attempt to satisfy the largest number of people's preferences. Citizens with similar preferences often organize interest groups in order to try to influence the actions of parties and policy-makers once they are elected. Individuals, interest groups, and public officials each may behave strategically, adjusting the orientation of their pressure tactics or coalition-building according to their perceptions of the activities of competing preferences. The aggregative model of democracy is problematic for a number of reasons. It undermines the ideal of democracy because it fails to give sufficient attention to the emphasis on effective participation and enlightened understanding, two criteria which deliberative democrats believe are vital for achieving a more just polity.

According to the aggregative model of democracy citizens participate in the decision-making process primarily by making their preferences known through voting. Voting is thus conceived of as the primary political act. But deliberative democrats reject this narrow conception of participation. To fully participate in the decision-making process, argue deliberative democrats, one must participate in authentic deliberation and not simply express one's preferences. Such deliberation requires that parties abandon the strategic behaviour characteristic of the aggregative model of democracy and strive instead to reach a consensus among free and equal participates.

To participate in this discursive practice is very different from participating in the decision-making process of the aggregative model of democracy. Deliberative democrats characterize participation in the democratic process as a transformative process. Through the process of public discussion with a plurality of differently opinioned and situated others, people often gain new information, learn of different experiences of their collective problems, or find that their own initial opinions are founded on prejudice or ignorance, or that they have misunderstood the relation of their own interests to others.

The more expansive conception of democratic participation that deliberative democrats endorse thus ties in well with the third criterion of democracy Dahl identifies—gaining enlightened understanding. A process of aggregating existing preferences precludes enlightened understanding as there is no attempt to understand, let alone accommodate, the concerns of one's fellow citizens. But deliberative democrats believe that their vision of democracy fosters enlightened understanding among citizens because it embodies the principle of reciprocity or the dispositions of reasonableness.

Elaborating on the former Gutmann and Thompson argue that reciprocity entails mutual respect. Mutual respect is a form of agreeing to disagree. It consists in an excellence of character that permits a democracy to flourish in the face of fundamental moral disagreement. This is a distinctively deliberative kind of character. It is the character of individuals who are morally committed, self-reflective about their commitments, discerning of the difference between respectable and merely tolerable differences of opinion, and open to the possibility of changing their minds or modifying their positions at some time in the future if they confront unanswerable objections to their present point of view.

By engaging in deliberation with those we disagree with we are expressing a willingness to listen to others, to take their concerns seriously and to find some common ground so that a just compromise can be achieved. Gutmann and

Thompson consider a number of contentious policy issues, ranging from abortion and trade policy to welfare policy, to illustrate how the deliberative process fosters enlightened understanding and moral accommodation. But mutual respect does not mean that we must always accept the claims of those we disagree with, but it does require that we listen to their concerns and that we justify our decisions by appealing to reasons we genuinely believe all reasonable persons could accept. Gutmann and Thompson provide an example from public education to illustrate this point.

In 1983 the board of education in Hawkins County, Tennessee adopted a basic reading series that was to be used in all public schools. The aim of this reading curriculum was to teach both reading skills and the values of democratic citizenship. But a group of fundamentalist Christian parents asked that their children not be required to use the books on the curriculum. The books conflicted with their religious convictions and the parents did not want their children to be exposed to other ways of life that conflict what the Bible says. Gutmann and Thompson identify the following specific parts of the curriculum that the parents objected to:

- a short story describing a Catholic Indian settlement in New Mexico, on the grounds that it teaches Catholicism;
- a reading exercise picturing a boy making toast while a girl reads to him on the grounds that "it denigrates the differences between the sexes" affirmed in the Bible;
- an excerpt from Anne Frank's Diary of a Young Girl, because Anne Frank writes that nonorthodox belief in God may be better than no belief at all; and

– a passage describing a central idea of the Renaissance as "a belief in the dignity and worth of human beings," because such a belief is incompatible with true religious faith.

After discussing the parents' objections and acknowledging the sincerity of the parents' religious beliefs the board rejected their request to exempt their children from reading the textbooks. But this decision was not arrived at by simply invoking a "show of hands" approach to public education that would consider only the relative bargaining power of the interests on either side. The principle of reciprocity requires that we take the parents' concerns seriously, which the school board did. But the reasons the parents wanted to exempt their children from the curriculum (e.g. to prevent their children from making critical judgements) are reasons that actually violate the principle of reciprocity, argue Gutmann and Thompson, and this is why the parents' objections are not acceptable.

The parents' reasoning appeals to values that can and should be rejected by citizens of a pluralist society committed to protecting the basic liberties and opportunities of all citizens. Keep in mind that the parents are trying to prevent schools from teaching their children to make critical judgements, to use their imagination, to exercise choice "in areas where the Bible provides the answer," and to consider the merits of the idea that all human beings have dignity and worth. If the parents were successful, their children (and perhaps others) would fail to receive the education that is necessary for developing their capacities as democratic citizens. The parents would deny the school board the authority to teach future citizens the skills and knowledge that are necessary for protecting the liberties and opportunities of all citizens, including the parents and their children themselves.

The board's decision was justified, argue Gutmann and Thompson, because the curriculum is a reasonable way for a public school system to teach democratic values. The reasons for rejecting the parents' wish to have their children exempted from the curriculum are thus public reasons, reasons that all parents, regardless of their conception of the good, can reasonably accept. This is very different from telling the parents that their objections are rejected simply because the majority of parents do not share their concerns. Gutmann and Thompson believe that the school board's decision to reject exemptions from the reading curriculum was a reasonable policy, despite the fact that no actual accommodation took place.

Mutual respect does not mean that we must always accept the claims of those we disagree with, but it does require that we listen to their concerns and that we justify our decisions by appealing to reasons we genuinely believe all reasonable persons could accept. We do not reject their demands out of hand simply because they are in the minority. By seeking terms of agreement that are acceptable to all, the deliberative model of democracy better secures two of Dahl's criteria for democracy—effective participation and enlightened understanding—than does the aggregative model of democracy. The emphasis on voting and bargaining, which are the central political activities of the aggregative model, are replaced by the emphasis on searching for a consensus, being open-minded and respecting, and even accommodating, your opponent's position. To participate in the consensus-building process envisioned by deliberative democrats is to engage in a transformative process.

Principles of Democracy

The fourth criterion of democracy that Dahl identified above was that there must be opportunities for exercising final control over the agenda. In particular, Dahl is concerned that a minority interest might be allowed to decide the political agenda if we do not ensure that constitutional arrangements satisfy this fourth criterion. Concern for this criterion easily fits into the deliberative conception of democracy which premises the legitimacy of law on the assent of all citizens. Jurgen Habermas, for example, maintains that 'only those statutes may claim legitimacy that can meet with the assent of all citizens in a discursive process of legislation that in turn has been legally constituted'.

Similarly Joshua Cohen claims that 'the fundamental idea of democratic legitimacy is that the authorization to exercise state power must arise from the collective decisions of the members of a society who are governed by that power'. By equating legitimacy with the outcome of an actual democratic process the deliberative democrat rejects the idea that the content of the law should be premised on substantive principles that are independent of such a process, such as Rawls's two principles of justice. Habermas, for example, claims that "all contents, no matter how fundamental the action form involved may be, must be made to depend on real discourses (or advocatory discourses conducted as substitutes for them)".

According to Habermas's democratic principle the only test for the legitimacy of laws is a procedural test. Statutory legitimacy hangs solely on whether a law has been enacted in the correct way, not on whether it fulfils some antecedently specified substantive normative criteria for goodness or rightness. So proceduralists like Habermas take seriously the fourth democratic criterion put forth by Dahl—that there be opportunity to exercise final control over the agenda. The agenda is not fixed or limited in advance by appealing to some independent moral argument, such as the principles that the parties in the original position would choose. But it is worth considering what a justice theorist like Rawls might say in response to this purely "procedural" conception of legitimacy.

Recall that Rawls himself, when constructing the original position, appeals to the idea of pure procedural justice. But why does Rawls construct a hypothetical original position in order to determine what the principles of justice are instead of simply saying that whatever principles people actually endorse by a "show of hands" should be deemed the principles of justice? Rawls would reject the latter proposal because there is no way of ensuring that a "show of hands" vote on the principles of justice would treat everyone as equals. Citizens could simply endorse principles that unfairly favour themselves. By invoking the veil of ignorance, for example, the original position helps better secure an impartial decision than might be the case if we simply decided what is just by asking for a show of hands.

The original position helps clarify what considerations should and should not determine what the principles of justice are. So one concern that can be raised against the proceduralist conception of legitimacy advocated by theorists like Habermas is that by subjecting the demands of justice to the democratic process proceduralists run the risk of legitimising unjust outcomes. If the majority of citizens democratically decide to limit the rights of a particular religious group, for example, then such a law must be construed of as legitimate by proceduralists because it was arrived at via a democratic procedure. Constitutional democrats will thus want to qualify Dahl's fourth criterion of democracy by stipulating that the opportunity for exercising final control over the agenda must be limited.

If the legislature has complete control over the political agenda then this could led to unjust outcomes. Rights, argue constitutional democrats, have priority over the democratic process and a purely procedural conception of legitimacy violates this requirement. Deliberative democrats can respond to this kind of concern in a number of different ways. They might argue that such an unjust outcome might occur in a democratic process where legitimacy is simply equated with the will of the majority in a "show of hands" vote but that is not what constitutes legitimacy for proceduralists like Habermas. In order for a law to be legitimate all must be able to consent to it and the minority in question would obviously not consent to such a measure.

The idealising requirements of Habermas's "discourse ethics" thus builds in protections for certain rights and opportunities that rule out the kind of repressive policy just mentioned. So even proceduralists like Habermas believe that it is necessary to build guarantees of basic liberty and opportunity into the ideal conditions of deliberation. Such measures are to be viewed as those necessary for a fair democratic process.

If the outcome of the deliberative decision-making process must meet with the assent of all participants then these participants have a right to express their views, challenge the claims of their opponents and have a say in the final decision. To engage in the deliberative process is to seek a consensus and persuade your opponents by argumentation, not force or coercion. Thus by committing oneself to deliberation one is already implicitly endorsing certain ethical principles, hence the reason why Habermas describes the theory as "discourse ethics". So even Habermas's procedural defence of legitimacy provides grounds for guaranteeing basic liberty and opportunity. But once proceduralists qualify criterion four in this way it appears that they must align themselves with constitutional democrats and agree that certain rights are taken off the political agenda.

By doing so they will be susceptible to the criticisms Waldron raised against Dworkin. Recall that Waldron was critical of judicial review because judges, like citizens, also disagree about rights. Waldron argues that we should not permit officials who are not elected nor accountable to resolve moral disagreements. Waldron's concern is especially problematic for deliberative democrats given their commitment to the idea that the legitimacy of law is based on the assent of all. So Dahl's fourth criterion of democracy presents something of a paradox for deliberative democrats. If they believe that all citizens should have final control over the agenda then little or no limits should be placed on democratic rule.

Yet the democratic process itself requires certain things be taken off the political agenda (e.g. certain rights) and thus limiting democratic rule is necessary if all are to be given the opportunity to exercise final control over the agenda. Procedural principles do not prescribe what the content of the laws should be but only the procedures (such as equal suffrage) by which laws are made and the conditions (such as free political speech) necessary for the procedures to work fairly. Some deliberative democrats argue that the principles of deliberative democracy are substantive as well as procedural.

Gutmann and Thompson are critical of the purely proceduralist approach advocated by Habermas because it does not capture the value of basic rights. Citizens value basic liberty and opportunity, and their mutual recognition by fellow citizens, for reasons other than the role of these values in democratic deliberation. In Democracy and

Disagreement Gutmann and Thompson defend an account of deliberative democracy that includes substantive as well as procedural principles. These substantive principles include basic liberty and fair opportunity and these principles are extended to persons not solely for the sake of democratic deliberation, but also for the sake of reciprocity, mutual respect and fairness. But if substantive principles, or even just procedural principles, are built into the deliberative account of democracy then it looks like deliberative democrats will need to engage in the same kind of armchair theorising that they criticise justice theorists for engaging in.

Indeed, echoing Shapiro's criticism of justice theorists, we could say that many democratic theorists now take it for granted that there is a correct answer to the question what principles of democracy we ought to affirm; that Habermas, Joshua Cohen, Gutmann and Thompson or someone else will eventually get it right. Much of the current debate between deliberative democrats is exactly this kind of armchair theorising. Different principles, procedural and/or substantive, are defended as the principles of democracy by democratic theorists yet these principles themselves are not the outcome of any real democratic process. For example, in "What Sort of Political Equality Does Deliberative Democracy Require?"

Jack Knight and James Johnson examine the different kinds of equality deliberative democrats should endorse. They argue that democratic deliberation 'requires equal opportunity of access to political influence'. Because deliberative democrats are concerned with the effects the social distribution of power has on effective participation in the deliberative process they themselves are engaged in an "equality of what?" debate in the same way that justice theorists are. And thus the gulf between theoreticians of justice and democracy seems to narrow significantly. Like justice theorists, deliberative democrats are concerned with the distribution of material resources.

The resources individuals command has an impact on their position in the deliberative process and thus deliberative democrats must consider the effects the social distribution of power and resources have on effective participation in the deliberative process. Even some proceduralists now endorse substantive principles. In "Procedure and Substance in Deliberative Democracy" Joshua Cohen, who was influential in formulating the procedural account of democratic legitimacy, argues that deliberative democracy presupposes substantive principles. He argues that the deliberative view accommodates a "principle of participation" the requirements of which are quite extensive.

According to that principle, democratic collective choice—institutionalizing the tie between deliberative justification and the exercise of public power—must ensure equal rights of participation, including rights of voting, association, and political expression, with a strong presumption against restrictions on the content or viewpoint of expression; rights to hold office; a strong presumption in favour of equally weighted votes; and a more general requirement of equal opportunities for effective influence. This last requirement condemns inequalities in opportunities for office-holding and political influence that result from the design of arrangements of collective decision-making.

Cohen's claim that the principle of participation entails a strong presumption against restrictions on the content or viewpoint of expression is particularly interesting given that is a rather specific claim about the content of law that is derived, not from a Kantian conception of the self, but from the idea of democratic legitimacy. It thus looks as though deliberative democrats who endorse substantive principles of democracy end up sharing more common ground with justice theorists like Rawls and Dworkin than one might have initially suspected given the former's desire to distance itself from the airchair theorising of justice theorists.

Both deliberative democrats and egalitarian-liberals are concerned with basic liberties, equality of opportunity and economic inequalities. But the reason deliberative democrats are concerned with these rights, opportunities and inequalities stems from their concern with principle of democratic legitimacy. Deliberative democrats are concerned with economic inequality, for example, not because they believe justice requires that we mitigate morally arbitrary factors or strive for an "ambition-sensitive"/ "endowment-insensitive" distribution, but because structural inequalities (e.g. social and economic power) threaten the ideal of deliberative democracy itself. Justice theorists could charge that deliberative democrats are simply caught up in a logical circle.

On the one hand these theorists do not want to posit an account of distributive justice that would pre-empt the decisions of the democratic process itself. Yet deliberative democrats do not wish to go along with the outcomes of existing democratic arrangements as these are ones that fail to live up to the idealising requirements of deliberative democracy. So deliberative democrats endorse substantive principles (e.g. the principle of participation) that must be satisfied before the outcome of the democratic process can be deemed legitimate yet it is exactly this kind of airchair theorising that democratic theorists criticise because they pre-empt the real democratic process as those principles are not ones that people have actually assented to.

Critical Edge of Deliberative Democracy

Some deliberative democrats have sought to salvage the ideal of deliberative democracy from the apparent assimilation to liberal constitutionalism. John Dryzek, for example, argues that deliberative democracy losses its critical edge when it is assimilated with liberal constitutionalism. Democracy is a dynamic and open-ended project and when the liberal state is seen as the key to facilitating authentic deliberation the changing empirical realities of the world are ignored. For example, Dryzek argues that the liberal state is increasingly subject to the constraints imposed by the transnational capitalist political economy.

The first task of all states in this system is to maintain the confidence of actual and potential investors, to avoid capital flight. This imperative conditions policy-making, for democratic influence on policy-making introduces a dangerous element of indeterminacy, and so becomes increasingly curtailed. Public officials under the sway of such imperatives are highly constrained when it comes to the terms of arguments they can accept; it is very hard for deliberation to reach them. In order to emphasis the critical strand of deliberative democracy Dryzek defends what he calls discursive democracy. Discursive democracy has the following characteristics:

1. It is pluralistic in embracing the necessity to communicate across difference without erasing difference.
2. It is reflexive in its questioning orientation to established traditions.

3. It is transnational in its capacity to extend across state boundaries into settings where there is no constitutional framework.

4. It is ecological in terms of its openness to communication with non-human nature.

5. It is dynamic in its openness to ever-changing constraints upon and opportunities for democratisation.

Iris Marion Young is another critical theorist who seeks to distance deliberative democracy from its more liberal variants. Young criticises Gutmann and Thompson for wrongly collapsing the value of justice into the value of democracy. Furthermore, Young argues that the principles that Gutmann and Thompson propose should govern the organization and conduct of deliberation-reciprocity, publicity and accountability—need to be supplemented by a principle of inclusion. The criterion of inclusion is the fifth and final criterion of democracy that Dahl identified above.

In the context of Dahl's analysis he simply means that all adults should have the full rights of citizens that are implied by the other four criteria. But the norm of inclusion, argues Young, requires that deliberative democrats reject some of their central assumptions. For example, that deliberation is culturally neutral and universal and that the process of discussion that aims to reach understanding must either begin with shared understandings or take a common good as their goal. This second assumption was implicit in Gutmann and Thompson's discussion of the school board's decision to reject the parents' argument for exclusion of their children from the curriculum.

After considering the central theses of the parents' argument Gutmann and Thompson argue that the board was justified because the parents request ran counter to the common good. The common good requires that we teach future citizens the skills and knowledge that are necessary for protecting the liberties and opportunities of all citizens. But if we assume unity as a staring point then the transformative dimension of deliberative politics is called into question. This is evident in the example Gutmann and Thompson consider. If we begin with the assumption that we all agree on the fundamental importance of protecting liberties and opportunities then it is easier to see how the board's decision is publicly justified. But if the deliberative process is suppose to be truly transformative, should we not also be prepared to question those initial opinions?

In other words, if we begin by appealing to shared understandings or take the goal of deliberation to be one of achieving a common good then we may leave little room for the transformative dimension of deliberative politics. In order to guard against this conservative consequence Young proposes seeing differences of culture and social perspectives as a resource which enriches the transformation of the deliberative process rather than something which must be overcome. She endorses a conception of communicative democracy that recognises the need for a more expansive conception of political communication, one that does not construe of argument in a culturally biased way.

The deliberative ideal tends to assume that when we eliminate the influence of economic and political power, people's ways of speaking and understanding will be the same; but this will be true only if we also eliminate their cultural differences and different social positions. Not all cultures express themselves in speech that is assertive and confrontational. If we are to ensure that the democratic process is inclusive of these other people and groups then we should not conceive of deliberation as a confrontation. This is the way Gutmann and Thompson present the case of the debate between the school board and the parents. Because the parents lacked a persuasive counter-argument to the proposal that their children learn these skills and knowledge they must concede defeat.

For deliberative democrats like Gutmann and Thompson the main concern is that disagreement should be resolved by the force of the better argument and not economic dependence or political domination. But if a determination of the "force of the better argument" itself privileges certain people then inclusion in the deliberative process is threatened. To guard against this exclusionary tendency Young suggests that deliberative democrats endorse an expanded conception of democratic communication, one that conceives of greeting, rhetoric and storytelling, in addition to argument, as contributing to political discussion.

Critical Assessment of Deliberative Democracy

Providing a critical assessment of the ideal of deliberative democracy is difficult for a number of reasons. Firstly, theorists from diverse traditions have allied themselves with the ideal and thus any criticism of deliberative democracy must distinguish between the subtle nuances of the different versions of that ideal. Secondly, because the deliberative turn in democratic theory is a recently new development there has not, at least as of yet, emerged a mass of critical literature on the theory. But we can raise a number of concerns which challenge both the appeal and viability of the deliberative model. These challenges are not meant to serve as a refutation of deliberative democracy but instead highlight some of the challenges proponents of this ideal must consider.

Let us begin with the concern that the emphasis on deliberation might have a destructive effect. Recall the example of the friends who were contemplating where to go for dinner. Whilst it might sound appealing for these friends to resolve their disagreement through a process of deliberation this process could undermine the very aim it was designed to resolve. Namely, to figure out where to go for dinner. The friends, who wish to be courteous interlocutors and thus give each participant a chance to air their concerns, could spend the whole night deliberating the pros and cons of the various restaurants thus skipping dinner altogether!

The transformative process of deliberation can be very time consuming and thus we must be able to say that there comes a point when more deliberation would not resolve disagreements, in fact, it might make things worse. So how much deliberation is enough? When does the virtue of efficiency, for example, trump the virtues of deliberation? If we have to wait till a consensus emerges before decisions can be deemed legitimate then we will never be able to make justified decisions about the pressing policy issues that face us in everyday politics, issues ranging from the economy and health care provisions to the environment and foreign policy.

The urgency to resolve some political disagreements thus threatens to undermine the priority deliberative democrats place on the value of "reasoning together". Environmentalists, for example, might welcome the opportunity to debate with their opponents the pros and cons of legislation that aims to limit gas emissions harmful to the environment. However, if environmentalists believe that immediate action is necessary to avert ecological disaster then they will view a prolonged discursive process as harmful, not beneficial. Sometimes we simply cannot afford to pursue, let alone wait for, a consensus to emerge before we act. Nor is it always possible to have a genuine open debate on certain issues.

As Daniel Bell notes, sound foreign policy, for example, does not readily lend itself to open debate. This point is very pertinent given the current debates about the war on terrorism that have ensued in the wake of the terrorist attacks on Sept. 11, 2001. Open and constructive debate requires public access to reliable information but if this information is only available to military and political elites then genuine debate on these issues will be hampered. To insist that this information be made public for the sake of having an open debate could compromise national security because it would reveal sensitive information (e.g. surveillance operations or tactics) that needs to remain secret for reasons of national security. So by making deliberation the focus of their account of politics, deliberative democrats run the danger of subordinating other important values, such as efficiency and security.

Deliberative democrats must make room for these other values if they are to avoid the criticism that they ignore the potentially destructive effects of deliberation. In order to avoid the pitfalls of deliberation Bell emphasises the preconditions that make constructive moral deliberations more likely. One of these preconditions is that deliberation is more likely to be effective if the political culture values decision-making by intellectual elites. This is so, argues Bell, "because talented elites with the motivation and the ability to understand and apply moral principles to complex political controversies with national (and international) implications are more likely to engage in constructive deliberations."

Bell claims that this is a relatively controversial precondition (in a Western context). Deliberative democrats are likely to reply that this is a very controversial precondition and will want to resist Bell's suggestion because it threatens to undermine the core of the idea of democratic legitimacy, namely, the idea that everyone whose basic interests are affected by policies should be included in the process of making them. But Bell's suggestion does highlight a dilemma the deliberative democrat must address. This dilemma is that the very things that make the ideal of deliberation sound inclusive, such as Gutmann and Thompson's principles of reciprocity, publicity and accountability, are the very same things that also threaten to make it exclusionary as most citizens will not have the information nor the capacities needed to satisfy these diverse demands.

Indeed the endorsement of deliberation itself has not emerged through a genuinely deliberative process. So there seems to be something undemocratic about claiming that ordinary citizens ought to engage in deliberative activity the terms of which are dictated by democratic theorists! This brings us to a second, related criticism, that the deliberative democrat must address—the charge that the ideal of deliberative democracy is utopian. Is it realistic to think that we can have both deliberation and mass participation? Critics could argue that, given the size of the population of modern democracies, talk of citizens engaging in genuine deliberation is just impossible.

Deliberative democrats might seek to address this concern by either restricting the number of occasions when popular deliberation should occur and/or by restricting the number of people involved in the deliberation. John Rawls, for example, employs both strategies. He narrows the range of issues that must be deliberated by claiming that public reason only applies to fundamental political questions, such as constitutional essentials and matters of basic justice. Furthermore, Rawls restricts the number of people involved in public reasoning by distinguishing between what he calls the "public political forum" and the "background culture". The former includes judges and government officials and candidates for political office. These individuals must engage in public reasoning when, for example, they decide legal cases or party platforms. But public reason does not apply to the background culture of society (e.g. civil society).

Rawls's strategy for dealing with the problem of large scale is unsatisfactory.

Firstly we must ask exactly which issues qualify as the "fundamental" issues to which the standards of public reason apply. If this list is construed of too narrowly then deliberative democracy will lose its transformative dimension as it seems that we can just appeal to the aggregative model of democracy to resolve most of the issues that come up in day-to-day politics as these issues will be deemed ones that do not raise fundamental political questions.

Secondly, it presumes that we can determine which issues are matters of "basic justice" independently of any genuine deliberation with others so we are back to the armchair theorising that democrats wished to distance themselves from.

Thirdly, if we believe that day-to-day politics does address fundamental political questions and thus think it is appropriate to hold them up to the deliberative standard then the problem of large scale is not resolved.

And finally, the democratic dimension of deliberative democracy is threatened by Rawls's division between the political forum and civil society.

If only judges and politicians are bound by the dictates of public reason then it seems that we have abandoned the core idea of deliberative democracy—the idea that everyone whose basic interests are affected by policies should be included in the process of making them. One novel suggestion that has recently been proposed as a way of making the ideal of deliberative democracy seem less utopian is that put forth by Bruce Ackerman and James Fishkin in "Deliberation Day". Ackerman and Fishkin suggest that a new national holiday be created called Deliberation Day. It will be held one week before major national elections.

Registered voters will be called together in neighbourhood meeting places, in small groups of 15, and larger groups of 500, to discuss the central issues raised by the campaign. Each deliberator will be paid $150 for the day's work of citizenship, on condition that he or she shows up at the polls the next week. All other work, except the most essential, will be prohibited by law. Deliberation Day is meant to serve as a "bottom-up" transformation of the democratic process. Contemporary politics is dominated by public opinion polling, sloganeering and sound bits as political candidates sell themselves like commodities.

One way of breaking this civically impoverished process is to improve the character of public opinion itself. Ackerman and Fishkin believe that many citizens actually want to take the public good seriously but the current arrangement does not have the necessary incentives in place to encourage this on a mass level. By paying deliberators for their efforts Deliberation Day will provide the incentives necessary to make such mass participation possible. But Ackerman and Fishkin believe that Deliberation Day will also generate a number of other incentives. Not only will it provide the social context necessary to engage in deliberation with other citizens, it will also transform the way political candidates run their campaigns.

In plotting their campaign strategies and advertising, politicians and their consultants would use Deliberation Day as a fundamental reference point. They would no longer automatically suppose that candidates were best sold in eight-second bites. Throughout the campaign, their eyes would be fixed firmly on the fact that their messages would be subjected to a day-long dissection—and that millions of votes might swing as a result. Ackerman and Fishkin cite the results of deliberative polls as evidence of the transformative potential of Deliberation Day. In these polls a random sample of people are first given a questionnaire that they answer regarding issues of public policy.

They then meet in small group discussions and larger plenary sessions and are given the opportunity to hear competing views and consider the evidence before making a final, more informed and reflective, decision. Engaging in extended dialogue about shared public problems often results in a dramatic change of opinion as compared to how people initially answered the questionnaire. Ackerman and Fishkin recognise that there would be problems with implementing a proposal like Deliberation Day but do not believe these obstacles are insurmountable. If deliberative democrats are seriously committed to both deliberation and mass participation then they must engage in the kind of innovative practical theorising exemplified by Ackerman and Fishkin.

The rise of the deliberative turn in democratic theory is important for at least two reasons. Firstly, it offers us an account of democracy that is not as civically impoverished as the aggregative model of democracy and one that coheres with the practices we often associate with a democracy (e.g.

open discussion and debate). And secondly, the deliberative turn in democratic theory has brought justice theorists and democratic theorists closer together.

The relation between justice and democracy is a complex and important relation and deliberative democrats force political theorists to take more seriously the question of how these two fundamental values are related.

8

Civic Socialisation

The democratic imperative was first spelled out by Thomas Jefferson and his colleagues as a lesson drawn from their study of the fate of earlier republics: citizens must be educated for a free nation to persist and prosper. They located the development of democratic citizens in the study of history, politics, and rhetoric, and they believed in the local control of schools, which should be encouraged and supported by leadership in the states. In the mid-19th century, Horace Mann and the founders of the public school movement developed the notion of the "school common to all people" with the explicit purpose, beyond intellectual development, of creating a common value system and a sense of community and harnessing the growing diversity of the citizenry.

In the pan-Protestant values they actually espoused, however, these schoolmen alienated Catholics and disparate others, who reacted by founding parochial and other private schools-which have persisted until the present as largely separate educational venues. Over the next hundred years, the schools were assigned a variety of social and democratic missions: to contribute to economic progress through agricultural and manual trades programs, to spearhead the

Americanisation of immigrants, and to help counteract the effects of industrialisation on children and communities.

More recently, the schools were given particular responsibility for overcoming the educational ill-effects of poverty and discrimination-providing equal educational opportunity and targeted instructional assistance but also preparing all students more effectively in terms of social development and the exercise of citizenship. As a consequence of this amalgamation of missions, public schools have had, for most of the last century, several broad, ill-defined, and contentious responsibilities:

- Impart the knowledge and skills of citizenship in an increasingly complicated polity.
- Inculcate a set of civic values-such as mutual respect and tolerance, fairness, honesty, generosity, and helpfulness-where there is no substantial consensus on their meaning and appropriate application in society.
- Prepare students for the practical dimensions of adult life and work through a "hidden curriculum" concerned with adaptation to economic life, orderliness, punctuality, persistence, and, more recently, teamwork.

The relative significance of these expectations is fiercely argued by persons with different value perspectives. And any or all of these outcomes are comprehended by various definitions of the social and democratic purposes of schooling embedded in current discussions of educational choice.

Caught in the cross fire of values that characterise these matters, educators have become increasingly loathe to express value-laden positions about the exact nature of the expected "democratic" outcomes. It is thus not surprising that the issue of civic socialisation has been mostly off the table throughout the course of the modern school-reform movement, beginning with A Nation at Risk. Academic achievement in reading and math have been the dominant outcomes sought; these are the desired outcomes in the voucher and charter discussions, too. Nevertheless, the issues remain highly significant to students, educators, and the general public.

A series of recent reports from Public Agenda show that large majorities of each group (typically between 60 and 90 percent) rate such attributes as honesty, tolerance, responsibility, hard work, and the habits of good citizenship as extremely important outcomes of schooling-more important than all subject matter learning; in fact, more important than anything except basic skills in reading and mathematics.

Although civic socialisation has not played a leading role in the movement for vouchers and charters, supporters have developed theoretical arguments that voucher and charter schools will be more effective than existing public schools in the advancement of democratic purposes. Among the advocates of vouchers, this view has perhaps been most prominent in the work of John Coons and Stephen Sugarman. They argue that the modern instruments of democratic control have produced a public-school curriculum that avoids or short-changes consideration of such essential public values as tolerance and civic responsibility. They also argue that autonomous, chosen voucher schools can acknowledge and build on legitimate differences in values that characterise America's pluralistic society without abetting abhorrent ideologies, particularism, or civic fragmentation.

Chester Finn, Bruno Manno, and Gregg Vanourek, meanwhile, predict that charter schools will recreate local democratic governance and thus help rebuild civil society around schools. Over the past two decades, in studies focusing mostly on Catholic schools, other scholars have developed an elaborate theory of the ways in which such schools' graduates should be well prepared for democratic citizenship. This theory has been most fully set forth by Anthony Bryk, Valerie Lee, and Peter Holland in Catholic Schools and the Common Good.

Building on the earlier work of James Coleman, Andrew Greeley, and others, and on their own field studies and analyses of national data sets, Bryk and colleagues argue that character formation of each student as a "person-in-community is the central educational aim" of Catholic schools. They go on to say: From this perspective, schooling involves more than conveying the acquired knowledge of civilisation to students and developing in them the intellectual skills they need to create knowledge. Education also entails forming the basic disposition for citizenship in a democratic and pluralistic society. A commitment to the pursuit of truth, human compassion, and social justice is essential to society's well-being. Fostering such a commitment makes serious demands on schools. If they are to teach children how they should live in common, they must themselves be communities. The school must be a microcosm of society-not as it is but as it should be.

Taken together, the theories of those sympathetic to or advocating choice seek to turn the conventional wisdom about the importance of the common school on its head: they suggest that choice schools would enhance rather than diminish the preparation of students for a democratic society.

Theories that are more skeptical of choice and supportive of the common school model of public education reach precisely the opposite conclusions. There have not been many formal theoretical defences of the democratic value of public education; its defenders have relied largely on rhetorical recapitulations and refinements of traditional common school notions, as well as lamentations about the insidious effects of individualistic market-oriented philosophies. By far, the most important theoretician among those apprehensive about choice has been Amy Gutmann, in Democratic Education and subsequent writings. Her view proceeds from a theoretical analysis of the requirements for a "democratic state of education," as distinguished from an education determined predominately by the state or by the preferences of families.

For Gutmann, the public interest in schooling manifestly involves education in citizenship, especially now, when political issues are complex and require citizens to have extensive knowledge and capacity for deliberation. Given the pluralism and diversity of society, she argues, the decision of which democratic values to teach can be made only through continual deliberations among diverse parties and perspectives. In her view, public control is the only way that this public interest may be fully expressed and protected.

For Gutmann, vouchers are inimical because they short-circuit democratic deliberation and undervalue the community's public interest in promoting citizenship. She argues that voucher programs place the vital decisions about appropriate democratic values beyond the influence of the community, creating an undemocratic "state of families," in which parents have excessive influence over the education of their children. Moreover, in counterpoint to Bryk, Lee, and Holland, other scholars have cautioned that the community values promoted in some religious schools may be incompatible with larger social goals. Law professor James Dwyer argues that religious schools promote narrow, authoritarian ideologies that are hostile not only to the healthy social and psychological development of their students, but also to tolerance and pluralism in a democratic society.

Challenges of Studying Civic Socialisation

The democratic performance of schools-whether public or private, choice or not-has not been much studied empirically. The first challenge associated with studying civic socialisation involves finding measures that can achieve consensus endorsement. Americans have long agreed on the importance of civic socialisation in the schools but not on the specific content of that socialisation.

We do not intend to settle debates about the content of the civic and democratic values that should be promoted in publicly funded schools. Nevertheless, we believe that there is sufficient consensus on these issues to describe, in general terms, the kinds of empirical outcomes that might be examined to assess school performance in promoting civic values. For example, most Americans would agree that all students (or graduates) should demonstrate:

- Civic knowledge about the formal operations of government, American history, and competing points of view on important political and policy issues.
- Civic attitudes that include tolerance and respect for diversity.
- Civic behaviour that includes voting and community participation, as well as the avoidance of criminal behaviour.

Policymakers need to know whether voucher and charter schools are more or less effective than conventional public schools at promoting these kinds of civic knowledge, attitudes, and behaviour, which are surely necessary aspects of healthy citizenship in a democracy. In fact, however, few reliable measures or benchmarks exist for any of these outcomes, nor have scholars developed substantial theories of what would constitute appropriate levels of performance.

Most of the existing voucher and charter evaluations have collected no data on student learning in the realm of civic socialisation, nor have they examined the democratic attitudes and behaviour of voucher and charter students. We are aware of only two exceptions, both involving privately funded voucher programs and both carried out by Paul Peterson and colleagues. The first of these, which examined a voucher program in the San Francisco Bay Area, used a telephone survey of a small number of students to assess their attitudes regarding tolerance of opposing views. The study found that voucher students in San Francisco were as tolerant as students who had applied for but not used vouchers.

As the authors recognise, however, these data are purely descriptive and cannot be used to make any kind of causal claim about the effectiveness of voucher schools in socialising citizens. Students were not randomly assigned to receive vouchers, so the comparison of voucher students and voucher applicants who remained in the public schools is likely to be plagued by selection bias.

The second evaluation, carried out by Peterson and David Campbell, assessed the effects of a voucher program initiated by the Children's Scholarship Fund (CSF) on a nationwide scale in 1999. This evaluation also relied on a telephone survey, but it had the advantage of random assignment: scholarships were awarded by lottery, creating a more appropriate control group of nonrecipients. Among a variety of other topics, the study examined, in five brief questions, students' political knowledge and tolerance.

On the tolerance measure, scores of the voucher students and the control group were very similar, and no significant differences were found. Voucher students answered the two civic knowledge questions correctly more often than their public-school counterparts did, but the differences were not statistically significant. Although these results do not support the fears of voucher opponents, we hesitate to give them much weight, because the measures are very thin and the results are very shortterm, based on only a single year of voucher experience. In sum, as of today, researchers and policymakers have very little convincing empirical evidence on civic socialisation outcomes in existing voucher and charter schools.

Civic Socialisation in Public and Private Schools

Lacking adequate socialisation data from voucher and charter programs, we turn to studies that examine civic socialisation in existing public and private schools. Most of the available empirical studies have sought to measure the civic performance of public or private schools and their students in relatively specific ways, using survey or interview techniques that cannot measure deep or long-term effects, and they have not been conducted in schools affected by voucher/ charter policies. Still, these studies may begin to provide suggestive information for the debate over vouchers and charters.

Using large-scale national data sets, recent studies of public- and private-school students found limited suggestions of an advantage for private-school students on some aspects of civic socialisation-or, as choice proponents emphasise, some reassurance that private schools do not foster the civic ignorance or undemocratic attitudes that many critics of charters and vouchers fear.

A study by Jay Greene that used data from the National Education Longitudinal Survey (NELS) found that, compared to their public school counterparts, private-school students, teachers, and administrators report greater levels of racial tolerance, less racial conflict, more volunteering (though not greater commitment to its importance), and a higher level of commitment and success in promoting good citizenship. This study controlled for differences in the socioeconomic status and race of public- and private-school populations, but did not adjust for unobserved prior differences in the values and attitudes of public- and private-school families, which may be substantial.

In consequence, it would be a mistake to conclude definitively that the measured differences are caused by privateschool attendance. Another study examined the civic activity and political participation of the parents of public- and private-school children. Controlling for a variety of background variables, it found that the parents of students in church-related private schools are more civically and politically active than other parents. Again, however, an attribution that the schools caused higher civic involvement is undermined by an inability to account for unobserved prior differences in values and attitudes. To date, the best study of the relationship between school sector and civic socialisation is David Campbell's multivariate analysis of the 1996 Household Education Survey.

Using several aspects of civic socialisation-including community service, civic skills, political knowledge, and political tolerance-Campbell compared students in conventional (nonchoice) public schools with students in public schools of choice (i.e., magnets et al., but not charters), Catholic schools, non-Catholic religious schools, and secular private schools. Because the Household Education Survey includes data on parents as well as students, Campbell's analyses were able to control not only for standard background variables including socioeconomic status and parental education, but also for measures of the civic participation and attitudes of parents.

Although selection bias remains a concern—the data are neither experimental nor longitudinal-the usual problem of unobserved differences should be less serious than in most studies, because many of the potentially important differences are "observed" in this data set and controlled in the analyses. Campbell also controlled for a number of school characteristics, including racial composition, school size, and the existence of a student government. Campbell's findings, comparing schools in each of the other sectors to conventional public schools, are as follows:

- Controlling for student, parent, and school variables (including the level of parental volunteering and whether the school requires community service), levels of community service are higher among students in Catholic schools by a statistically significant margin. Also, there are no statistically significant differences among the other school sectors.
- For civic skills-controlling for student, parent, and school variables
- there is a small but statistically significant advantage for students in Catholic schools; other sectors have results comparable to those of conventional public schools.

- For political knowledge-controlling for student, parent, and school variables – Catholic-school students have a statistically significant advantage and there are no statistically significant differences for other sectors.
- For political tolerance-controlling for student, parent, and school variables (including the political tolerance of parents) – there is a statistically significant advantage for students in nonreligious private schools, a statistically significant disadvantage for students in non-Catholic religious schools, and no statistically significant differences among the other sectors.

Summarising these findings across sectors, then, Campbell found:

- No significant difference along any aspect of civic socialisation between conventional public schools and public schools of choice (e.g., magnets).
- Advantages for Catholic schools in community service, civic skills, and political knowledge, and no significant difference between Catholic schools and conventional public schools in political tolerance.
- An advantage for secular private schools in political tolerance, and no significant differences between these schools and conventional public schools in community service, civic skills, or political knowledge.
- Less political tolerance among students in non-Catholic religious schools, though no statistically significant differences between these schools and conventional public schools in community service, civic skills, or political knowledge.

It would be a mistake to make too much of these findings. In the absence of an experimental manipulation or longitudinal data, attributing causation to the measured school-sector effects is problematic. But even if the positive findings for Catholic and secular private schools are discounted, opponents of choice will find little here to support their concerns-with the notable exception of the finding of lower tolerance in non-Catholic religious schools. In sum, although several studies find that private-school students (or their parents) score relatively well in terms of some measures of civic participation, knowledge, and attitudes, existing research is far short of being able to provide a causal attribution of those outcomes to attendance in private schools. Unfortunately, data on civic socialisation outcomes have not received nearly as much sophisticated methodological attention as data on student achievement in public and private schools.

Civic Socialisation in Catholic Schools

It is worth considering the effectiveness of Catholic schools in particular in promoting civic socialisation, for more than one reason. First, as we have seen, Catholic schools play a prominent role in all of the existing voucher programs. Second, Campbell's findings suggest the possibility that Catholic schools may have unique advantages in terms of promoting civic socialisation. Third, intensive case study research has led some scholars to conclude that Catholic schools exhibit a communal organisation promoting a strong focus on socialising students into communal values. The empirical work of Bryk, Lee, and Holland suggests that Catholic schools manifest (vis-à-vis public schools) several characteristics that promote a communal environment that might contribute toward effective civic socialisation:

- They demonstrate a positive school climate and a shared school culture.

- As a matter of strong conviction, they avoid bureaucratisation and seek to build a local school community.
- They are safer and more disciplined.
- They develop high orders of identity and self-esteem in their students, attributes shown to promote tolerance.
- They afford more-frequent and more-intensive opportunities for student service.
- In their efforts at character formation, they see themselves as "bridges" to adult life in society with an emphasis on the virtues of mutual obligation and trust-key ingredients in the formation of social capital.

Although these characteristics might plausibly be related to civic socialisation, Bryk and colleagues have been primarily interested in their influence on outcomes such as teacher commitment (e.g., efficacy, morale, absenteeism) and student engagement (reduced class cutting, disorder, absenteeism, and dropping out). Their direct influence on civic attitudes, values, and knowledge remains, for now, only speculative.

9

Citizenship Identity and Civic Education

Citizenship is a core identity. As citizens, people develop a sense of belonging to a country and a community. They are aware of and adopt the norms and values that are endemic to their culture. There is hardly a consensus about the meaning of democratic citizenship in the academy or in practice. The construct of the citizen in the United States is highly contested, and historically has undergone a variety of manifestations. This contestation is evident in the various decisions civic educators have made about what essential attributes of citizenship should be fostered.

Civic education can promote particular citizenship ideals based on the attributes of citizenship that are advanced. The variations in perspectives on civic education mirror in many ways the core points of contestation in academic studies of political socialisation. Research on political socialisation can be construed as providing a report card on the status of civic education at particular points in time. It also to a great extent reflects the priorities of civic educators, including their assumptions about what makes a good citizen.

In an effort to shed light on the complex issues of what essential attributes of civic education are being promoted in the United States and which attributes should be fostered, it is useful to begin by briefly examining the nexus between civic education in practice and political socialisation scholarship. This examination reveals three dominant, somewhat overlapping, constructs of the citizen that have undergirded political socialisation scholarship and the teaching of civic educators.

Citizenship constructs that specify a more expansive role for the citizen in society have become more prevalent. However, conveying even the most fundamental knowledge that forms the basis upon which citizenship orientations build remains a challenge, even as civic educators strive to reformulate their mission to meet the increasing demands on citizens in an evolving and complex political culture.

Civic Education and Social Science

Gimpel, et al., provide a standard definition of political socialisation as, "the process by which new generations are inducted into political culture, learning the knowledge, values, and attitudes that contribute to support of the political system". Civic education is an element of the political socialisation process that involves the active development of citizenship orientations in young people. The intellectual origins of political socialisation research are positioned within debates about civic education. These debates focused heavily upon issues of pedagogical practice until the 1930s.

The emphasis within academia then began to shift from training citizens to empirical investigations into the development of citizenship orientations. More recent trends are moving in the direction of integrating research and practice. Political science emerged as a discipline in the mid-nineteenth century as part of an educational reform movement sparked by the need to deal with social and political problems in the wake of the Civil War and the growing complexities of the state. Some political scientists believed that it was the discipline's moral responsibility to educate good democratic citizens and leaders.

The dominant position within the academy since the 1880s, however, hardly was enlightened or optimistic about the possibilities of civic education for the mass public. Ball contends that throughout the Wilsonian movement, the Progressive period, and the behavioural revolution, political scientists, regardless of their theoretical or methodological differences, were united in their "concern-or perhaps preoccupation-with the (in)capacity of citizens to govern themselves". Reflecting on the ability of scientific investigations of politics to shed light on theoretical questions of democratic participation, Pool lamented that most studies of civic culture and socialisation focused on people who are less trustful of the polity, less participatory, less interested, and less confident of their power to change things than social scientists think they ought to be. This observation might easily have been made today.

During the Wilsonian era, this position was manifested in the belief that the discipline of political science should act as a agent of social control serving the state, especially by training specialists in leadership and administrative science, and by producing academic researchers. Ball's description of Woodrow Wilson's attitude toward mass civic education provides great insight into the prevailing views within political science from the 1880s through the Progressive period and even beyond. "Wilson saw citizens much as a teacher sees his unkempt charges. A little learning and a lot of discipline can go a long way toward chastening high-spirited democrats, damping down their enthusiasm, and banking the fires of radicalism".

Political scientists during the Progressive period, in keeping with the idea that average citizens were incapable of playing more than a marginal role in democratic governance, sought to expose political corruption and proposed reforms. The goal was to make boss politics and political machines less appealing to the masses, and not to enhance civic involvement. Civics texts, which were often aimed at assimilating the growing immigrant population, downplayed the need for active participation in the political realm, and instead stressed cultural myths, such as those associated with America dream of unlimited opportunities for all who worked hard.

The emphasis during these phases of the discipline's development fell more heavily on the production of civil servants than on teaching civics to the general public. Charles Merriam's landmark work in the 1920s and 1930s provided the impetus for the emergence of political studies of socialisation and at the same time sought to further the practical enterprise of civic education. Merriam and his colleagues produced a series of cross-cultural investigations which examined the development, control, and implications of civic training in eight nations-Austria-Hungary, England, France, Germany, Italy, Russia, Switzerland, and the United States.

These works provided a point of departure for studies focusing on the relationship between political socialisation and political regimes. They identified the specific qualities of citizenship that were being taught across nations. These included patriotism and loyalty, obedience to the law, respect for government and public officials, individuals' recognition of their political obligations, a minimum degree of self-control, responsiveness to community needs in stressful times, knowledge of and agreement with the legitimating national ideology, and a recognition of the special qualities of people within one's country compared to those of other nations.

Missing from this itemisation is the notion that good citizens must be able to exercise judgement about political problems, policies, and ideas. Merriam, reflecting the position of John Dewey, considered critical thinking to be an essential characteristic of a good American citizen, and was concerned that civic education was not developing such skills. Merriam's work promoted the importance of systematically educating democratic citizens to a generation of scholars, although the widespread implementation of his ideas both in terms of establishing a vital research agenda and instituting civic education programs in the classroom were far from realised in his day.

He identified a broad range of agencies involved in the civic education process, privileging the school and agents of popular culture, especially newspapers, radio, and film. He downplayed the role of the family, an agent that came to loom too large in subsequent investigations. Merriam importantly noted that the political is constantly interacting with the nonpolitical, and that political values only make sense within the larger context of the individual in society.

Political socialisation scholarship flourished during the behavioural period in political science beginning in the late 1950s, while the discipline's concern with the actual education of citizens subsided. Behaviouralism's inherent emphasis on objective scientific analysis was at odds with the concerns about practical pedagogy that preoccupied political scientists of an earlier era, including Merriam and Wilson. The dominant research methodologies employed by socialisation scholars, especially survey research, created greater distance between the citizen (subject) and any real world educational goals.

Hands-on approaches to assessing the value of particular civic education initiatives generally were avoided. A spate of studies during the 1980s indicating the declining civic engagement of young Americans sparked a resurgence of interest in civic education within the academic community. Research findings showed that people under the age of thirty-five pay less attention to politics and have lower levels of political knowledge than older people. Young people distrust politicians and have limited faith in government institutions to act in the best interest of citizens.

Younger citizens are less inclined to register and turn out to vote in elections than their senior counterparts. They are unlikely to work on a candidate's campaign or for a political party, contact a public official about a policy issue they care about, or attend a political meeting to express their views. In reaction to these findings, a healthy trend developed within the American scholarly community to unite research and practice in endeavours to increase civic competence among young people.

Constructions of the Citizen

Civic education and political socialisation scholarship have left a legacy of stock citizenship constructs. These include the citizen as loyal subject and patriot, the citizen as voter, and the citizen as enlightened community participant. These constructs, while not mutually exclusive, prioritise particular attributes that conform to specific notions of the good citizen.

Early political socialisation research objectives maintained the importance of stable political regimes, and focused on formal processes of teaching and learning designed to foster regime support. The concern with transmitting regime norms across generations led to an early emphasis on preadults as the primary targets of civic education. Training focused on children learning the basic information, values, and beliefs about politics that are necessary for their later role as adult citizens. The impetus behind this perspective is articulated in Merriam's fundamental question, "How much economic pressure, or ethnic pressure, or religious or cultural pressure is necessary to induce the patriot to change his allegiance?". This view of the citizen hinges on the idea of civic loyalty as fostered by the state and potentially undermined by allegiances to groups operating outside the governmental realm.

The use of systems models is fundamental to socialisation research in this vein. Landmark studies focused on early education as the source of learned support for the political system. Of particular concern was how patterns of loyalty to authority, obedience, and conformity are established. It is essential for the citizen as loyal subject to learn about the customs, traditions, rituals, folklore, and heroes that are part of a nation's political culture, and which are passed on generationally. In addition, citizens need to acquire knowledge of the formal rules, such as the country's constitution and codified laws, as well as the unstated rules, for example, the willingness in the United States to accept the outcomes of elections without resorting to violence.

Consenting to core American values is a cornerstone of this citizenship construct. These values include egalitarianism and individualism, as well as those vested in the American creed which emphasise the exceptional nature of the nation's development and its special place in the world. Instilled in good citizens is a belief in the rule of law, the idea that government is based on a body of law, agreed upon by the governed, that is applied equally and justly. These values contribute to the public's diffuse support or high degree of respect for the American system of government and the structure of its political institutions.

Other core values passed on through civic education and socialisation include patriotism, the love of one's country and respect for its symbols and principles, and political tolerance, the willingness to allow groups with whom one disagrees to exercise their constitutionally guaranteed freedoms, such as free speech and assembly. The Citizen as Voter Three decades ago, Dawson and Prewitt observed that certain aspects of political socialisation, such as how American children acquire their partisan identification and voting related orientations, have been studied extensively, while other areas have been virtually ignored.

Some scholars and practitioners consider political socialisation to be synonymous with instilling norms related to voting behaviour. Niemi and Hepburn acknowledge this fact: "Given our emphasis on both preadults and young adults, the boundaries between political socialisation, public opinion, and voting behaviour are likely to be ill-defined and permeable.... We do not see it as a problem". Underlying the citizen as voter construct is the assumption that voting is the single most important political act in a democracy.

The consistently low level of voter turnout among young people is viewed as cause for alarm, as it signals that younger generations do not have a strong conventional sense of civic duty. As a result, civic education prioritises values and activities associated with participation in elections with the goal of motivating young people to vote when they come of age. Successfully socialising young people to be future voters is challenging, as it is difficult to translate abstract political duties into concrete political orientations and actions.

Civic education efforts need to engage students in meaningful exercises that provide them with direct experience in the electoral realm, even if voting is not an option. A drawback of the citizen as voter construct is the implicit assumption that by voting citizens are fulfilling there political responsibilities. It may not be either desirable or necessary for the mass public to participate beyond this "simple" act.

Young people's declining interest in political affairs, especially government service, over the course of the past two decades has prompted civic educators to focus on preparing young people to become responsible participants in the community. This perspective emphasises "enlightened political engagement" as an essential component of citizenship. Essential to the socialisation of citizens is the recognition of a shared connection to community that requires adherence to democratic norms.

The practice of citizenship is associated with a sense of responsibility that guides participation for all members of society. The enlightened citizen focus requires young people to acquire knowledge about how the political system works and to develop the skills needed to keep informed about government and public policies. They also need to acquire community problem-solving skills, which have been demonstrated to instill in young people the belief that they can make a difference and to stimulate volunteerism.

In an increasingly complex world, the challenges for civic education are compounded, as evidenced by the requirements of an enlightened citizen. Civic education must convey the basics about the Constitution, government and political processes to provide young people with a foundation of knowledge that can serve as a source of political empowerment. In 2004, junior high and high school civics and history classes fall far short of teaching even the basics about the Constitution or the U.S. system of government. That leaves a tall order for civic educators seeking to promote enlightened engagement.

Young people must gain the civic skills necessary for participation. Importantly, they must be able to critically assess and develop an understanding of politics without giving in to cynicism and alienation. Changing notions of what constitutes a hero in American society can provide insights into the challenges civic educators face in the current environment. In addition to the difficulties they have in instilling the basics, they face competition from other agents who promote values and behaviours, however inadvertently, that run counter to citizenship ideals. Heroes embody the human characteristics most prized by a country, and are a meaningful component of a nation's civic identity.

A nation's political culture is in part defined by its heroes who, in theory, embody the best of what that country has to offer. Heroes can act as civic educators because they are role models for people throughout the life course, especially youth. Traditionally, heroes were people who are admired for their strength of character, beneficence, courage, and leadership. Today, people are more likely to achieve hero status because of other traits, such as celebrity, athletic excellence, and the ability to earn a great deal of money.

Shifts in the people a nation identifies as heroes reflect changes in cultural values. Prior to the twentieth century, political figures were preeminent among American heroes. These included patriotic leaders, such as American flag designer Betsy Ross, prominent presidents, like Abraham Lincoln, and military leaders, such as Civil War General Stonewall Jackson, a leader of the Confederate army. People learned about these leaders from biographies which provided information about the valiant actions and patriotic attitudes that contributed to their success.

10

Rights of the Individual

In December 1998, the United Nations marked the 50th anniversary of the world's most comprehensive human rights declaration: the Universal Declaration of Human Rights (UDHR). As a whole, the document was meant to recognise the inherent dignity and equal rights of all human beings. In essence, the document represented the basic needs, hopes, and wishes of men and women around the world. A review of the thirty articles of the UDHR reveals a commitment to education, health, work, and culture as well as legal and political rights:

- Article 1: Right to equality
- Article 2: Freedom from discrimination
- Article 3: Right to life, liberty, and safety
- Article 4: Freedom from slavery
- Article 5: Freedom from torture and cruel, inhumane punishment
- Article 6: Right to be protected by the law
- Article 7: Right to be treated in the same way as others by the law
- Article 8: Right to legal aid if rights are not respected

- Article 9: No arbitrary arrest, prison, or exile
- Article 10: Right to a public and fair trial
- Article 11: Right to be considered innocent until proven guilty
- Article 12: Right to privacy and protection
- Article 13: Right to move within one's country and to leave/return to it when one wishes
- Article 14: Right to protection in another country if one's rights are violated in one's own country
- Article 15: Right to be a citizen of one's own country or to become a citizen of another country
- Article 16: Right to marriage and family
- Article 17: Right to own property
- Article 18: Freedom of religion
- Article 19: Freedom of opinion and speech; freedom to give and receive information
- Article 20: Right to organise meetings
- Article 21: Right to participate in government and in free elections
- Article 22: Right to personal development by taking part in the economic, social, and cultural life of the country
- Article 23: Right to work for fair pay and to join labour unions. Right for women to receive pay equal to men's pay
- Article 24: Right to paid holidays and reasonable work hours

- Article 25: Right to food, housing, and medical care
- Article 26: Right to an education
- Article 27: Right to participate in the cultural life of one's community
- Article 28: Right to a social and international order that protects all these rights
- Article 29: Community duties are necessary for free and full development of people
- Article 30: Right to all these freedoms without interference by government or individuals

The thirty articles of the UDHR were written and agreed upon by representatives of many different nations, nations with different political systems and different populations. The United Nations was not the first organisation to promote respect for human rights. In 1791, for example, the Constitution of the United States of America was amended to include a Bill of Rights. The Bill of Rights, in actuality the first ten amendments to the U.S. Constitution, was created to protect the basic rights of U.S. citizens. As an example, the first amendment protects individuals from governmental interference by means of freedom of speech, press, assembly, and religion.

Amendments five to eight define and protect specific rights of individuals accused of crimes or involved in disputes under law; more specifically, the sixth and seventh amendments guarantee an individual's right to a lawyer and a trial by jury. Since the passage of the Bill of Rights in the late 1700s, an additional 17 amendments have been added to the U.S. Constitution. For example, slavery was outlawed in 1865 with the 13th amendment; women were granted the right to vote in 1920 with the 19th amendment;

and in 1971, the minimum voting age in the U.S. became 18 with the passage of the 26th amendment. Other nations have passed similar declarations to recognise and protect individual rights. Sadly, many people around the world find themselves living in environments without the rights set forth in the UDHR some fifty years ago.

One way to keep the ideals of the Universal Declaration of Human Rights alive and to promote their importance is to integrate them into education. Language teachers can create many different content-based lessons around the Universal Declaration of Human Rights, the Bill of Rights, and the concepts underlying these declarations.

Lesson Planning

Materials: Create two sets of handouts, with four different versions of each. Each handout in the first set should include five provocative statements, each one related in some way to at least one of the articles in the Universal Declaration of Human Rights (UDHR). The goal is to include statements that are likely to stimulate meaningful and extended discussion among students. For more advanced students, teachers might want to include the original UDHR articles; for less proficient students, even more simplified versions could be included.

Student grouping decisions: Decide on procedures for grouping students for Activities #1 and #2. If appropriate, make up tentative lists of group members for each activity. It is recommended that groups have no more than six participants each. Make last minute adjustments when it is determined which students are actually in class.

Vocabulary considerations: Consider the vocabulary that students need to know to complete the lesson successfully.

Determine which vocabulary items the students already know and which items they'll need to be introduced to.

Warm Up Activity

Purpose:

- To stimulate student interest in the topic of individual rights
- To tap students' background knowledge
- To introduce vocabulary that will facilitate successful completion of the lesson

Procedures:

1. Write "Universal Declaration of Human Rights" on the blackboard.
2. Ask students what the Universal Declaration of Human Rights is. Put key words from students' responses on the blackboard. If students are unfamiliar with the Universal Declaration of Human Rights, be prepared to provide students with relevant background information, adding words to the blackboard as you introduce key ideas.
3. Underline the word "Rights" on the blackboard. Ask students what "rights" might be included in the declaration. Add key words and concepts to the blackboard.

Transition from Warm Up to Activity #1

Tell students that the class session will be devoted to exploring aspects of the Universal Declaration of Human Rights.

Activity #1 (approximately 25 minutes)

Purpose:

- To provide students with opportunities to use English in a meaningful way
- To introduce students to the Universal Declaration of Human Rights in relation to real-world situations
- To give students the chance to use key vocabulary and concepts associated with the theme of the lesson

Procedure:

1. Divide students into four groups (A, B, C, D) in the quickest way possible. The number of groups that you actually have will depend largely on the size of your class. For example, with a small class, all students in group A can sit together. With a large class, you can create multiple A groups, multiple B groups, multiple C groups, and multiple D groups.
2. Working alone, students should read each statement on their handout and indicate with a check ( ) whether they strongly agree (SA), agree (A), are uncertain (U), disagree (D), or strongly disagree (SD) with the statement. If students have never engaged in an exercise like this, put an example sentence on the blackboard to model the process in front of the entire class. Ask students to be ready to explain the reason for their responses to classmates. While students are working individually, circulate among them to make sure they understand all important vocabulary and the task at hand.
3. Ask students to be ready to explain the reason for their responses to classmates. While students are working individually, circulate among them to make sure they

understand all important vocabulary and the task at hand.

4. Ask students to discuss their responses with members of their group (A, B, C, or D). Ask students to do the following (if necessary, write instructions on the blackboard):

   a. Compare your responses with group members.

   b. Explain your reason for each response.

   c. Ask group members questions if you do not understand their reasons.

While students are working in groups, circulate around the classroom. Make sure students stay on task. Answer questions and/or provide clarification when needed.

5. Distribute Handout #2; give appropriate version (A, B, C, or D) to each group. Ask students to do the following:

   a. Match each situation on Handout #1 to the appropriate Universal Declaration of Human Rights article(s).

      While students are working together, circulate and provide them with feedback on their responses, referring to the Answer Key for reference. Point out key words which might help them with the matching exercise.

6. Ask groups to identify the situation and UDHR article which caused the most discussion (or controversy, debate, interest) among them. Tell students to be prepared to explain group selection (and reasons for the selection) to other students in class.

Activity #2 (approximately 15 minutes)

Purpose:

- To provide students with opportunities to use English in a meaningful way
- To reinforce key vocabulary and concepts associated with the theme of the lesson
- To give students the opportunity to be successful in English by asking them to report information discussed earlier with other classmates

Procedures:

1. Create new student groups--ideally with at least one representative from original groups A, B, C, and D--in the fastest way possible.
2. Ask students to do the following in their new groups:
   a. Identify the situation and Universal Declaration of Human Rights article which caused the most discussion (controversy, debate, interest) in original group.
   b. Explain diverse opinions of classmates.
   c. Answer questions from new group members.

Cool down activity (approximately 5 minutes)

Purpose:

- To provide some closure to lesson
- To give students an opportunity to discuss relevance of lesson

Procedures:

Look back at blackboard. Ask students the following questions:

a. What words can we add to the blackboard to create a more complete picture of the Universal Declaration of Human Rights? Add students' responses to the blackboard.

b. Which concepts are most controversial? (Circle students' responses.)

c. Which concepts are most interesting? (Box students' responses.)

d. Which concepts are most important? (Put a star next to students' responses.)

e. Why are they important?

Possible Extensions to Lesson

1. Ask students any of these questions to extend the lesson.

   a. Which UDHR articles do you find most interesting? Most important? Least important? Why?

   b. Are universal standards, such as those listed in the UDHR, possible in today's world? Why? Why not?

   c. Do you think the United Nations should enforce the UDHR? Why? Why not?

   d. What would society be like if everyone followed the UDHR?

   e. Why do you think so many nations have not been able to live up to the Universal Declaration of Human Rights?

2. Remind students that the UDHR was written in 1948, in response to the events of World War II and the global depression of the 1930s. Ask students to

consider these two questions: Which UDHR articles, if any, are no longer needed today? What new articles need to be added to the Declaration to respond to today's life and world situation?

3. Ask groups of students to select one article of the UDHR that they feel is important. Give groups time to plan a presentation about the UDHR article that they've selected, in the form of a poster, skit, song, poem, or essay. While students make their presentations, their classmates should be asked to guess which UDHR article the group is highlighting.

4. Ask students to work in groups to draft a "Declaration of Individual Rights for the 21st Century." Students should be prepared to defend and provide a rationale for their choices. Have students compare their drafts and generate a final "Class Declaration of Individual Rights."

FREEDOM OF EXPRESSION

Classroom Applications

Lesson Planning

Materials: For Activity 2, compile sets of three scenarios--highlighting issues related to individual freedoms--for each group of students.

Student grouping decisions: Decide on procedures for grouping students for Activities 1 and 2; participants will remain in the same groups for both activities. It is recommended that groups have no more than six participants each. If appropriate, make up tentative lists of group members. Make last minute adjustments when it is determined which students are actually in class.

Vocabulary considerations: Consider the vocabulary that students need to know to complete the lesson successfully. Determine which vocabulary items the students already know and which items they will need to be introduced to.

Warm Up Activity (5-10 minutes)

Purpose:

- To stimulate student interest in the topic of individual freedoms
- To draw upon students' background knowledge
- To introduce vocabulary that will facilitate successful completion of the lesson

Procedures:

1. Write the following list of five freedoms on the blackboard:
   - Freedom of speech
   - Freedom of press
   - Freedom of assembly
   - Freedom of religion
   - Freedom of conscience
2. Ask students what comes to mind when they think about these freedoms. Write key words and phrases, from student responses, on the blackboard next to each freedom.
3. Ask students if they want to add other individual freedoms to the list on the blackboard. If students

respond to your request, ask contributors to define the freedom for their classmates. Put key words on the blackboard.

Transition from Warm Up to Activity #1

Tell students that the class session will be devoted to exploring the individual freedoms listed on the blackboard.

Activity #1 (approximately 15-20 minutes)

Purpose:

- To provide students with opportunities to use English in a meaningful way
- To rank order individual freedoms and come to a group consensus on the importance of different freedoms
- To give students the chance to use key vocabulary and concepts associated with the theme of the lesson

Procedures:

1. Ask students to work individually to rank the freedoms listed on the blackboard from most important (1) to least important (5). (If students have expanded the original list of five freedoms to include new items, the number associated with the least important category will have to change so that one number can be assigned to each freedom on the blackboard.) Remind students that there are no right or wrong answers. Circulate while students are completing their rankings to make sure everyone completes the assignment; help students who are having difficulties.
2. Assign students to groups. Ask groups to do the following:

a. Discuss and compare rankings

b. Explain reasons for ranking decisions

c. Agree on a group ranking; come to a group consensus

Circulate in the classroom while student groups are working. For groups that have difficulties reaching a consensus, ask them to try to agree on only the most and least important freedoms. For groups that finish much earlier than other groups, ask them to identify the most controversial freedoms and to discuss the nature of the controversies.

3. Ask volunteers from each group to report on group decisions. Focus on those freedoms considered to be most important and least important. As each group reports to the class, record responses on the blackboard by putting a check plus (+) next to the freedoms considered most important and a check minus (-) next to the freedoms considered least important. If time permits, ask group members to provide a rationale for their decisions.

Do not erase the blackboard. Come back to it at the end of the lesson as a way to provide meaningful closure to the lesson.

Activity #2 (approximately 20 minutes)

Purpose:

— To provide students with opportunities to use English in a meaningful way

— To reinforce key vocabulary and concepts associated with the theme of the lesson

– To explore the intricacies of the freedoms listed on the blackboard

Procedures:

1. Ask students to think about the freedoms listed on the board. Should the freedoms ever be limited? When? Under what circumstances?

2. Ask students to consider the following situation: A teenager, in a movie theater, yells "fire" even though there is no fire.

   a. Should the teenager be allowed to yell, "fire"? Why? Why not?

   b. Which freedoms are being questioned here?

3. Ask students to work in their original groups. Give each group a set of three (or four) scenarios. For each scenario, students should consider the following questions:

   a. Which freedom(s) is being questioned?

   b. Should the freedom be limited? Why? Why not?

4. As students are beginning to finish up their group discussions, ask each group to identify the most controversial scenario.

5. Ask a volunteer from each group to comment on the most controversial scenario to classmates from other groups.

Cool down activity (approximately 5 minutes)

Purpose:

– To provide some closure to lesson

- To give students an opportunity to discuss relevance of lesson

Procedures:

1. Remind students that, at the beginning of class, they identified certain freedoms as being more important than others are. Point to freedoms marked with a check plus (+) on the blackboard. Ask students if they still agree with their original decisions. Ask for comments.
2. If time permits, ask students to think about the class session on individual freedoms. Pose questions such as the following:
   a. What did you learn in class today?
   b. What differences in opinion did you hear today?
   c. Should some individual freedoms be limited? If so, under what conditions?

Possible Extensions to Lesson

1. Ask students any of these questions to extend the lesson.
   a. Why is it important to protect freedom of expression: freedoms of speech, press, assembly, religion, and conscience?
   b. Why are restrictions of freedoms based on time, place, and manner sometimes necessary?
   c. How does the principle of "separation of church and state" relate to individual freedoms, in particular, freedom of religion?
   d. What can a society do to find a proper balance between individual freedoms and the rights and interests of the larger society?

e. Why do you think so many nations have not been able to live up to the Universal Declaration of Human Rights?

2. Ask groups of students to write up new scenarios that highlight the discord between individual freedoms and societal interests. They can be asked to present the scenarios to their classmates, identify the freedom(s) involved, and explain possible restrictions.

3. Ask students to list (and then present) arguments in favour of and against an individual freedom.

Freedom of the Press

Proponents of freedom of the press cite numerous benefits including the following:

1. It promotes individual growth and human dignity; the right to express one's ideas and communicate with others contributes to one's growth as a person. The right to consider other people's views and opinions also contributes to individual growth.

2. It is important for the advancement of knowledge; new and improved ideas are likely to be developed in societies that allow free discussion, debate, and the consideration of multiple perspectives.

3. It is a necessary component of representative governments; freedom of the press is crucial in both determining policy and checking how well governments carry out their responsibilities.

4. It facilitates peaceful social change; the right to express oneself freely provides an outlet for individuals trying to influence public opinion by persuasion rather than violence.

5. It is essential for the protection of all individual rights; the ability to express oneself allows people to speak out against the violation of one's rights by others or by the government.

The challenges related to freedom of the press, however, are many. When contemplating freedom of the press, one must consider if and when limits and restrictions are advisable.

Classroom Applications

Preliminary lesson planning

Materials: Create a handout for Activity 2. Add news items to the list (or adjust those that are currently listed) to stimulate student discussion and debate.

Student grouping decisions: Decide on procedures for grouping students for Activities 1 and 2; participants will remain in the same groups for both activities. It is recommended that groups have four participants each. If a large class size makes groups of four unrealistic, form larger groups. The lesson plan suggests that each member of the group be assigned a special role (e.g., chairperson, recorder, reporter, responder). For larger groups, be prepared to assign additional roles such as a checker of understanding (one who makes sure everyone in the group understands what is being done and said); a cheerleader/encourager (one who offers encouragement and praise for contributions of group members); a turn-taking monitor (a person who makes sure all members participate); a voice/noise monitor (a person who asks students to either speak up or speak more quietly). If appropriate, make up tentative lists of group members. Make last minute adjustments when it is determined which students are actually in class.

Vocabulary considerations: Consider the vocabulary that students need to know to complete the lesson successfully. Determine which vocabulary items the students already know and which items they will need to have explained.

Warm up activity (5 minutes)

Purpose: To draw upon students' background knowledge

Procedures

1. Ask students the following question: Where can we get information about local, national, and world news? List student responses on the blackboard. (Possible student answers include newspapers, news magazines, television, radio, the Internet, friends, and family.)
2. Before asking the next question, add "1st choice" and "2nd choice" to the blackboard so that the blackboard looks something like this:

1st choice	2nd choice
Newspapers	News Magazines Television Radio Internet Friends Family

3. Conduct an informal class survey. Ask students "Which news sources do you prefer? What is your first choice? What is your second choice?" Read off each news information source listed on the blackboard, one at a time, and ask students to raise their hands if it is their first choice, and then their second choice. Put tally marks in each column.
4. Ask students to examine the results of the informal class survey. Ask them "What news sources do we prefer as a class?" Circle the news sources that students most commonly use.

Transition from Warm Up to Activity #1

Tell students that this class session will focus on one individual freedom. Ask them "Which individual freedom do you think we will be talking about today?" Try to elicit freedom of the press from them. Define the term, if necessary. Relate student responses to the notion of freedom of the press.

Activity #1 (approximately 15-20 minutes)

Purpose:

- To provide students with opportunities to use English in a meaningful way
- To give students the chance to use key vocabulary and concepts associated with the theme of the lesson
- To hold students responsible for their own learning

Procedure:

1. Put students into groups of four. Have students in each group choose numbers from 1 to 4 and then give them their role assignments:
   - Chairperson (leads group discussion)
   - Recorder (writes down group's ideas)
   - Reporter (reports group deliberations to the rest of the class)
   - Responder (answers questions from the whole class after the group report)
2. While students are forming their groups, erase the "1st choice" and "2nd choice" headings and tally marks from the board. Replace them with new headings, as indicated below:

	Reliable		Biased		Truthful	
	Most	Least	Most	Least	Most	Least
Newspapers						
News Magazines						
Television						
Radio						
Internet						
Friends						
Family						

Also write the following questions on the blackboard:

A. Which news source is the most reliable? Least reliable? Why?

B. Which news source is the most biased? Least biased? Why?

C. Which news source is the most truthful? Least truthful? Why?

3. Ask students to work in their groups to answer these questions. Before they begin to work together, make sure they understand the three key terms: reliable, biased, and truthful. Remind students that they should be able to defend their responses to these questions. Give students a time limit (about 10 minutes).

4. Ask reporters to report on group deliberations. While reporters are speaking, record their answers with check marks ( ) on the blackboard. Encourage other class members to ask responders for clarification. Put these questions on the blackboard to encourage and model appropriate questioning: How did your group come to that conclusion? Why does your group feel that way? How can your group defend that answer?

5. Ask the class if any of the news sources that are listed limit or restrict their reports about local, national, and world news. Ask the class why news is sometimes limited or restricted. Write student responses on the blackboard. (Student answers might include national security, number of stories to report, time or space limitations, politics, privacy, protection of the innocent, protection of people's reputations, secrecy, fear, power.)

Activity #2 (approximately 20-25 minutes)

Purpose:

- To provide students with opportunities to use English in a meaningful way
- To reinforce key vocabulary and concepts associated with the theme of the lesson
- To encourage students to take a stand in English about important issues
- To give students an opportunity to defend their opinions in English

Procedures:

1. Ask students to remain in the same groups. Assign new roles to students, using these guidelines:
   - Recorder (writes down group's ideas)
   - Reporter (reports group deliberations to the rest of the class)
   - Responder (answers questions from the whole class after the group report)
   - Chairperson (leads group discussion)

2. Distribute one copy of the News Reports handout to each group. Go over instructions, introduce new vocabulary, and if necessary, review key vocabulary.

3. Have students work in their groups to answer questions on the handout. Give students a time limit (about 10 minutes) to keep them on task.

4. Ask reporters to report on group deliberations. Encourage other class members to ask responders for clarification. Refer back to the questions on the blackboard to encourage/model questioning: How did your group come to that conclusion? Why does your group feel that way? How can your group defend that answer?

Cool down activity (approximately 5 minutes)

Purpose:

– To provide some closure to the lesson

– To give students an opportunity to discuss relevance of the lesson

Procedures:

1. Ask students to review what happened in class. ("What have we done in class today?")

2. Ask students "How is today's lesson related to freedom of the press?" (Help students understand the intricacies associated with freedom of the press. Freedom of the press does not simply give individuals the ability to report whatever they please, it also grants individuals the power to choose what to report, what not to report, and the extent, tone, and manner of reporting.)

Possible Extensions to Lesson

1. Ask students any of these questions to extend the lesson.

   a. Who is responsible for reliable journalism: journalists, editors of newspapers, directors of radio stations, the government?

   b. Should all citizens have equal access to information? Why? Why not?

   c. What should the public know to be considered informed citizens?

   d. Should newspapers and radio stations be able to report whatever they want? Why? Why not?

   e. How has public access to information changed in the last decade in our country? Are these changes positive or negative? Why?

2. Ask students to list and present their arguments in favour of and against freedom of the press.

3. Ask students to imagine that they are the directors of the evening news for a popular local television station. Their job is to choose stories for the evening news, a 15-minute broadcast featuring local stories. Tell them that four of the 15 minutes are dedicated to commercials, giving the students a total of 11 minutes of news time. They can combine three different story lengths: 30-second spots, 60-second stories, and 2 ½ minute (150 second) features. Give students a list of at least 20 "headlines" to choose from. Have students plan the evening news by creating a programme schedule with three columns:

   Column one: List the news items in order of presentation (1, 2, 3, etc.);

Column two: Identify the length (spot, story, feature) of each news item (for a total of 11 minutes);

Column three: State the reason(s) for choosing the news for this position and length.

11

Civics Education Framework

Civic responsibility is comprised of actions and attitudes associated with democratic governance and social participation. Actions of civic responsibility can be displayed in advocacy for various causes. By advocating social issues or environmental concerns, people strengthen their commitment to their community as well as to their own individual citizenship. Some attitudes related to civic responsibility include the intention to serve others, the belief that helping others is ones social responsibility, and the tolerance and appreciation of human differences.

Students enrolled at institutions of higher education have the opportunity to transform their social interests into advocacy through personal connections with the community. Higher education has been commissioned to teach the values of a democratic society. These democratic values honour individual diversity, the common good of the larger community, and the active enterprise of social improvement. A variety of higher education policy statements have been written that discuss civic responsibility and the potential impact of social participation on students.

Historically, higher education has been viewed as a vehicle to promote holistic student development. Included in holistic development is the component of civic responsibility. The Student Personnel Point of View, An American Imperative: Higher Expectations for Higher Education, the Student Learning Imperative, and the Declaration on the Civic Responsibility of Higher Education are policy statements that reflect the importance of civic responsibility in higher education.

U.S National Civics Framework Assessment

The National Assessment of Educational Progress (NAEP) is a survey mandated by the U.S. Congress to collect and report information about student achievement in various academic subjects, such as mathematics, science, reading, writing, history, geography, and civics. The National Assessment Governing Board (NAGB) sets policy and the overall dimensions for the assessment programme. NAGB has scheduled a National Assessment in civics for 1998 to gauge knowledge and skills about civics and government of the nation's 4th-, 8th-, and 12th-grade students.

Citizenship—commitment to and participation in a community's civic life—is the engine of constitutional democracy and a free society. Knowledge of the rights, responsibilities, and privileges of citizenship fuel that engine. Without the participation of informed, effective, and responsible citizens, a democratic republic cannot and does not function, nor can it make progress toward its ideals. It is important, therefore, that Americans understand the civic values on which the nation was founded and by which it has since been guided.

It is also important to assess young people's knowledge of civics and their understanding of the principles by which the nation does and must govern itself. Any increase in citizens' civic knowledge, skills, and participation strengthens our republic; any reduction in their knowledge, skills, and participation weakens it. Thus, civic education is central to American education and essential to the well-being of American constitutional democracy. To gauge the civic knowledge and skills of the nation's 4th-, 8th-, and 12th-grade students, an assessment has been scheduled for 1998 by the National Assessment of Educational Progress (NAEP) in U.S.

A biennial, congressionally mandated survey, NAEP sometimes is called "The Nation" Report Card" because for more than 25 years it has collected and reported survey-based information about student achievement in mathematics, science, reading, writing, history, geography, and other subjects, including civics. NAEP is not a national test; however, it is a barometer or broad indicator of how much and how well students are learning. It is not used to gather information on individual students, nor is it a basis for sanctions or rewards in the education system. In accordance with law, NAEP does not report scores for individual students or schools.

The National Assessment Governing Board (NAGB), NAEP's policymaking body, oversees the activities of each assessment and is authorised by Congress to determine the content of the assessment. To prepare for the 1998 assessment of civics, this Framework, or set of guidelines, has been developed through an extensive, national, consensus-building process involving experienced educators, scholars, students, and citizens from many walks of American life. The purpose of this Framework is to:

- Specify civic knowledge and skills that students at grades 4, 8, and 12 should possess and on which they should be assessed.
- Describe the desired characteristics and approaches of the 1998 assessment of civics.
- Present preliminary descriptions of the three levels of achievement—basic, proficient, and advanced—by which students' performance will be judged and reported in that assessment.

Achievement standards, the criteria by which students's command of knowledge and skills in specific academic subjects is measured, are becoming increasingly important. Voluntary standards in disciplines such as mathematics, geography, and civics have been produced at the national, state, and local levels, and curricular frameworks derived from them continue to be developed. These standards provide guidelines for teaching, learning, curriculum development, and teacher preparation, as well as for the writing of textbooks and instructional materials. As voluntary professional standards become reference points for schools, it is important that NAEP take them into account in designing the content and approaches of its assessments.

Furthermore, the National Assessment Governing Board's policy mandates that the content of the Nation's Report Card" reflect voluntary national standards appropriately. That is, each assessment should measure the effectiveness of practice both as it is and according to new voluntary standards, as it ought to be. The first edition of voluntary national standards for civic education, the National Standards for Civics and Government, was completed and published by the Center for Civic Education in 1994. The Standards's widespread favourable reception and their general approval by public agencies, professional educational institutions, and schools has allowed them to be a major, subject-matter reference point for planning the 1998 Civics Assessment, providing a focused and forward-looking direction for civic education.

In addition, other existing standards, curriculum frameworks, and assessments from states and school districts, as well as the significant literature concerning civic education, have been reviewed and considered in planning for the 1998 Civics Assessment. A review indicated that state practices and directions are moving toward the new National Standards for Civics and Government and that state plans for improving civic education are generally consistent with one another. The National Standards for Civics and Government and this NAEP Framework embody a broad consensus on what is of enduring significance in the discipline of civics and what students at grades 4, 8, and 12 should know and be able to do. These two documents constitute a set of challenging expectations; they are intended to signal the importance of ensuring high quality civic education for all students.

The 1998 assessment assumes that substantial progress already has been made toward the goals reflected in the national and state standards and this Framework. If a second assessment of civics were to occur sometime beyond the year 2000, even greater progress should be reflected.

International Assessment of Civic Education

An international assessment of civic education being conducted by the International Association for the Evaluation of Educational Achievement (IEA) is scheduled to occur concurrently with the NAEP Civics Assessment in

1998. Involving about 15 to 20 countries, the IEA assessment will consist of two phases. The first phase will be a descriptive profile or case study of civic education in each of the participating countries, including the United States. The second phase will be an assessment of student knowledge and skills in civics and government in each participating nation. The coincidence of the two assessments offers several opportunities and benefits for the NAEP assessment. The profile prepared for the international project should offer important contextual information for NAEP. The potential exists for the national and international assessments to be linked so that achievement data from the United States and variables influencing student performance may be compared with international findings.

The 1998 NAEP Civics Consensus Project began in February 1995 with the award of a contract by the National Assessment Governing Board to the Council of Chief State School Officers (CCSSO). Subcontracts were awarded to the Center for Civic Education (CCE) and the American Institutes for Research (AIR). A national consensus-building process took place over the course of the following year. A planning committee composed of teachers, curriculum specialists, teacher educators, assessment experts, and lay people drafted this Framework.

The Planning Committee's work was guided by a Steering Committee made up of representatives of key education and policy organisations augmented by members from business, government, and the general public. Both the Planning and Steering Committees benefited from advice obtained through public hearings, student forums, and written reviews of successive drafts of this Framework. During the planning process, NAGB provided support and guidance through its staff and Subject Area Committee #1.

The NAEP Civics Framework document is supplemented by three other technical documents "Civics Assessment and Exercise Specifications, Recommendations for Background Questions, and Reporting Recommendations" which provide additional recommendations and criteria by which the assessment will be developed and the standards by which civic knowledge and skills will be assessed and reported.

The National Assessment of Educational Progress in civics in 1998 is a welcome development for several reasons.

First, the National Education Goals proclaim, "By the year 2000, all students will leave grades 4, 8, and 12 having demonstrated competency over challenging subject matter including... civics and government... so tha they may be prepared for responsible citizenship, further learning, and productive employment... All students will be involved in activities that promote and demonstrate... good citizenship, community service, and personal responsibility."

Second, there is growing public awareness of the need for and the importance of civic education as evidenced in recent opinion polls.

Third, policymakers who appreciate the utility of reliable information about students' learning at critical junctures of their school experiences, realise that a decade has elapsed since the last civics assessment. Still another reason that the scheduled assessment is important is its potential to sustain the momentum created by the publication of national and state standards for civics and government.

All of those involved in the development of the forthcoming civics assessment are keenly aware that its ultimate significance will depend upon the extent to which it can be used to improve instruction and increase learning. By providing fair, accurate, and timely information on student achievement at the national and state levels to the public, policymakers, and educators, this assessment can affect improvement in civic education for all of America's children. That students are well prepared for citizenship is a matter of importance to them as individuals and to our society as a whole and to the maintenance and improvement of our constitutional democracy.

Civic education in a constitutional democracy is the preparation of citizens to fulfil their responsibilities to sustain and enhance self-government. Democratic self-government in the United States requires citizens to participate in the affairs of their communities, state, and nation. To participate effectively, citizens need intellectual and participatory skills, as well as knowledge about their government and society. Acquisition of civic knowledge and skills makes possible a reasoned commitment to those fundamental values and principles essential to the preservation and improvement of American constitutional democracy.

Many institutions help to develop Americans's knowledge and skills and shape their civic character and commitments. Families, religious institutions, the media, business, and community groups exert important influences. Schools, however, bear a special and historic responsibility for the development of civic competence and civic responsibility. Schools can and should provide effective civic education through both formal and informal means from the earliest grades through high school. From the time of the nation's founding, knowledge of government and civic life has been considered to be central to the endurance of the United States as a democratic republic.

Thomas Jefferson believed that an uneducated citizenry was a contradiction in terms.

John F. Kennedy, recalling the old saying that the course of civilisation is a race between catastrophe and education, insisted that in a democracy such as ours "we must make sure that education wins." Despite a national consensus on the need for civic education in elementary and secondary schools, this vital part of students' education is seldom given sustained and systematic attention in the K-12 curriculum. Inattention to civic education stems principally from the assumption that the knowledge and skills citizens need emerge as by-products of the study of other subjects or as an outcome of the process of schooling itself rather than as a consequence of a focused study of civics. As most studies of civic knowledge and dispositions show, this is not so.

The goals of democratic civic education are proclaimed in mission statements and curriculum guides of school districts and state departments of education. Civic education practices in schools, however, often do not measure up to these proclamations. Examination of civics curricula, instructional practices, and earlier assessments of civic knowledge reveal that:

- Although civics and government are often included as elements of social studies instruction in grades K-8, substantial treatment of those subjects is unusual.
- American history courses tend to emphasise social history and devote insufficient time to political history, such as the nation's founding period and subsequent constitutional development.
- Fewer than 25 states require secondary school students to complete at least a one-semester course in civics or

government, although school and district requirements at the local level may be higher.

– Assessments of student achievement in civics by national, state, and local education agencies tend to be inadequate and infrequent.

It also is apparent that the neglect of civic education in the schools has negative consequences for American students, schools, and society. Principally, this has been evidenced by unacceptably low levels of student achievement in measured knowledge of civics; voter turnout, particularly by citizens aged 18-24; and adult participation in civic life. For example:

– The 1988 NAEP Civics Report Card revealed that students tended to have only a superficial knowledge of civics; furthermore, the knowledge of civics that they did possess had declined since 1976.

– The same Report Card indicated disturbing disparities in achievement among some subpopulations. The achievement of white students tended to be significantly higher than that of Black and Hispanic students; and males were more likely than females to achieve the highest levels of civic proficiency.

– The 1995 nationwide appraisal of the attitudes and dispositions of first-year college students conducted by the UCLA (University of California at Los Angeles) Higher Education Institute revealed that the percentage of college freshmen who said that paying close attention to political affairs is important had declined to just 15 percent, its lowest level in 30 years.

– Membership records of such diverse organisations as the PTA, the Elks Club, the League of Women Voters, the Red Cross, labour unions, and even bowling leagues have declined by roughly 25 to 50 percent over the past two to three decades, according to research conducted by Robert Putnam of Harvard University in 1995 and 1996.

Despite these negative reports about civic knowledge and participation, several promising and positive trends are emerging throughout the nation. In fact, the negative reports are at least partially responsible for the increased interest by the public in incorporating into the school curriculum greater attention to civic education. At the Second Annual White House Conference on Character Building for a Democratic, Civil Society, held in 1995, members of the Task Force on Civic Education drew attention to some of the more positive trends. For example:

- Increasing numbers of policymaking bodies are reaffirming that effective civic education is essential to successful schooling.
- State and local curriculum framework documents are beginning to reflect the content and concepts embodied in the voluntary National Standards for Civics and Government.
- Civics and government courses in the nation's schools are becoming more substantive; they are incorporating more content from such formal disciplines as political science, law, economics, political philosophy, and history.
- Curricula in civic education reflect greater concern for the international context of public affairs and for the comparative analysis of political, economic, and legal systems.

- Interest in encouraging students to provide volunteer service to the community and in a more formal service learning curriculum is growing.
- Elected officials, representatives of civic organisations, lawyers, judges, law enforcement personnel, and other community resource people are volunteering more often to assist educators in teacher training and student activities.

The first national assessments, administered by NAEP in 1969-70, were in science, writing, and citizenship. In the ensuing years, civics was assessed four more times—1972, 1976, 1982, and 1988. Two of those assessments were conducted as a part of the assessment of the whole field of the social studies. In 1988, however, attention focused solely on civics and government, as will the forthcoming assessment.

Table 1: Previous NAEP Assessments of Civics and Citizenship

Subjects	*Years*
Citizenship	1969-70
Social Studies (including Citizenship)	1971-72
Social Studies (including Citizenship)	1975-76
Citizenship and Social Studies	1981-82
Civics: U.S. Government and Politics	1988

The most recent civics assessment, conducted in 1988, measured students's understanding of:

- The purposes of democratic government and of the principles expressed in basic American documents, such as the Declaration of Independence and the U.S. Constitution, including the Bill of Rights.

- The three branches of government and the organisational principles by which they function.
- The mechanisms by which citizens and politicians reach decisions and transform these decisions into political action.
- Rights, responsibilities, and the law—the specific rights and liberties guaranteed under the U.S. Constitution and the relationship between laws and rights.

The 1988 assessment was administered in approximately 1,000 public and private schools to a representative sample of more than 11,000 students in grades 4, 8, and 12. At grade 4, the assessment was composed of multiple-choice questions. At grades 8 and 12, the test was composed of multiple-choice questions and one con-structed-response item. Students also completed a questionnaire that elicited demographic information about themselves and about their experiences in studying civics and government. These background variables and performance data were analysed to reveal patterns of learning about civics and government. Because the most recent survey of civic education will be 10 years old in 1998, the National Assessment Governing Board has decided that a new assessment of students' knowledge of the subject should be undertaken.

Plans for the new assessment have been influenced by growing public concern about the condition of American government and of civil society' the sphere of voluntary individual, social, and economic relationships and organisations that, although influenced by law, is not part of the nation's formal governmental structure. The 1998 assessment, planned in response to this public concern, is designed to provide Americans with the first measure in a decade of students' knowledge of civics and of the skills of American citizenship.

Civic education is central to American education and to the well-being of American constitutional democracy. Civic education also is important to civil society—that historically essential sector of society composed of nongovernmental voluntary, community, fraternal organisations, clubs, and religious institutions. Sustained and systematic attention to civics, government, and civil society in the K-12 curriculum enables students to build on the knowledge they acquire in each successive grade. Therefore, students' understanding of civic life, politics, and government should increase both in scope and depth as they progress through the elementary, middle, and high school years. In addition, their command of essential intellectual and participatory skills should continue to develop as they move toward the assumption of the full rights and responsibilities of citizenship.

The 1998 Framework for the National Assessment of Educational Progress in civics has three interrelated components: knowledge, intellectual and participatory skills, and civic dispositions. Taken together, these components should form the essential elements of civic education in the United States. Development of a NAEP assessment of student achievement in civics, therefore, should fully reflect the need to evaluate students' command of these three components of civic education. The knowledge component, the core of this framework, is embodied in the form of five significant and enduring questions. These are questions that have continued to engage not only political philosophers and politicians; they are questions that do—or should—engage every thoughtful citizen. The five questions are:

1. What are civic life, politics, and government?
2. What are the foundations of the American political system?
3. How does the government established by the Constitution embody the purposes, values, and principles of American democracy?
4. What is the relationship of the United States to other nations and to world affairs?
5. What are the roles of citizens in American democracy?

The intellectual and participatory skills component of civic education involves the use of knowledge to think and act effectively and in a reasoned manner in response to the challenges of civic life in a constitutional democracy. Intellectual skills enable students to learn and apply civic knowledge in the many and varied roles of citizens. These skills help citizens identify, describe, explain, and analyse information and arguments as well as evaluate, take, and defend positions on public policies. Participatory skills enable citizens to monitor and influence public and civic life by working with others, clearly articulating ideas and interests, building coalitions, seeking consensus, negotiating compromise, and managing conflict.

The third component of this Framework, civic dispositions, refers to the inclinations or "habits of the heart," as de Tocqueville called them, that pervade all aspects of citizenship. In a constitutional democracy, these dispositions pertain to the rights and responsibilities of individuals in society and to the advancement of the ideals of the polity. They include the dispositions to become an independent member of society; respect individual worth and human dignity; assume the personal, political, and economic responsibilities of a citizen; abide by the "rules of the game," such as accepting the legitimate decisions of the majority while protecting the rights of the minority; participate in civic affairs in an informed, thoughtful, and effective manner; and promote the healthy functioning of American constitutional democracy.

The acquisition of knowledge and skills and the development of civic dispositions take place within a variety of contexts. Those of home, school, community, state, nation, and the world are especially important in civic education. They constitute the primary arenas in which citizens acquire knowledge and skills as well as put their knowledge and skills into practice.

Knowledge Component

It is important that all students have an opportunity to consider the essential questions about government and civil society that continue to challenge thoughtful people. Although there are various ways of phrasing these questions, this Assessment Framework follows the National Standards for Civics and Government in organising them in five major categories. What follows is a general description of these five broad content areas that are to be assessed.

Civic life, politics, and government

Citizens need to understand civic life, politics, government, and civil society so that they can make informed judgments about what government should and should not do, how they are to live their lives together, and how they can support the proper use of authority or combat the abuse of political power.

— Civic life is the public life of citizens concerned with affairs of the community and nation as contrasted with private or personal life, which is devoted to the pursuit of private and personal satisfactions.

- Politics is a process by which people reach collective decisions that are generally regarded as binding and enforced as common policy.
- Government may be described as the formal institutions and processes of a politically organised society with authority to make, enforce, and interpret laws and other binding rules about matters of common interest and concern, such as society's order, security, and prosperity. The term government also refers to the group of people, acting in formal political institutions at national, state, and local levels, who exercise decision-making power or enforce laws and regulations. Some parts of government such as Congress, state legislatures, and city councils make laws; other parts, including federal, state, and local agencies such as taxation authorities and police, enforce laws; and still others, such as federal and state courts, interpret laws and rules.
- Civil society refers to the complex network of freely formed, voluntary political, social, and economic associations. Among the many nongovernmental actors making up civil society are groups such as parent-teacher, professional, and business associations, labour unions, religious, charitable, and youth organisations, and social and fraternal clubs. A vital civil society is an essential component of a constitutional democracy, because it prevents the abuse or excessive concentration of power by government. The organisations of civil society also "are public laboratories in which citizens learn democracy by doing it."

At the early elementary level, students may begin to understand government and civil society by analogy with the governance of the family and school. As they progress through school, their knowledge and understanding of civic life, politics, and government should increase and deepen.

Foundations of the American political system

The American political system is based upon the values and principles of constitutional democracy expressed in such fundamental American documents as the Declaration of Independence; the U.S. Constitution, including the Bill of Rights; the Virginia Statute for Religious Freedom; the Federalist Papers; and Antifederalist writings. Other documents that express and elaborate upon the values and principles of the founding documents include the Seneca Falls Declaration of Sentiments and Resolutions, Martin Luther King? Letter from Birmingham City Jail, and landmark U.S. Supreme Court decisions. Such fundamental expressions of American principles and values are important for students to understand for several reasons.

First, Americans are a people bound together by the ideals, values, and principles they share rather than by kinship, ethnicity, or religion, which are ties that bind some other nations of the world.

Second, Americans' ideals, values, and principles have shaped their political institutions and affected their political processes.

Third, the ideals, values, and principles set forth in the nation's core documents are criteria that Americans use to judge the means and ends of government, as well as those of the myriad groups and organisations which are part of civil society.

Finally, understanding of fundamental principles provides the basis for a reasoned commitment to the ideals, values, and principles of American constitutional democracy.

The values and principles of American constitutional democracy are sometimes in conflict, and their very meaning and application are often disputed. For example, although most Americans agree that the idea of equality is an important value, they may disagree about what priority it should be given in comparison with another value, such as liberty. And they may disagree on the meaning of equality when it is applied to a specific situation. In addition, disparities have always existed between the realities of daily life and the ideals of American constitutional democracy.

Citizens should thus be encouraged to consider that while the history of the United States has been marked by continuing attempts to narrow the gap between the nation's ideals and reality, it has also achieved a wide degree of consensus as to what those ideals are and what that reality ought to be. It is on the basis of these ideals that Americans have united in political movements to abolish slavery, extend the voting franchise, remove legal support for segregation, and provide equality of opportunity. Citizens should be familiar with historical and contemporary efforts in which Americans have joined forces to work toward the achievement of their shared ideals.

Americans, however, realise that the United States is not Utopia, nor is a constitutional democracy Utopian. Rather, a constitutional democracy is a way of allowing the competing ideas, values, goals, and interests of people, individually or in groups, to compete with one another in a peaceful manner. A constitutional democracy affords its citizens means of reconciling their differences and their competing visions of truth without resorting to violence or oppression. Students in the early grades should become acquainted with the basic values and principles which are the foundation of the American political system. Their knowledge and understanding should increase as they progress through middle and high school.

Principles of American democracy

The system of government established by the Constitution has resulted in limited government and a complex dispersal of powers. As a result, Americans live under the jurisdiction of national, state, and local governments, all of whose powers and responsibilities are separated and shared among different branches and agencies. Each of these governments—national, state, and local—affects directly the daily lives of all Americans: their security, their opportunities, their standard of living, and the taxes they pay.

The Framers of the Constitution saw this complex system as a principal means of limiting the power of government. Multiple levels of government provide numerous opportunities for citizens to participate in their own governance. The system also reflects the principle of popular sovereignty, enables citizens to hold their governments accountable, and helps to ensure the protection of the rights of individuals. Citizens who understand the justification for this system of limited, dispersed, and shared power and its design are able to evaluate, monitor, and influence it more effectively.

To understand the impact of the various levels of government on their daily lives, the lives of their communities, and the welfare of the nation as a whole, students need to understand how local, state, and national governments are organised, what they do, and how they interact.

Relationship of the United States to World Affairs

The United States does not exist in isolation; it is part of an interconnected world in whose development it has played and continues to play an important role. The American political tradition, including the ideas expressed in the Declaration of Independence, the U.S. Constitution, and the Bill of Rights, has had a profound influence abroad. The nation's democratic ideals and the benefits of its free society have drawn the attention and inspired the hopes of people worldwide. In addition, the United States has exerted extensive economic, technological, and cultural influence on other nations. At the same time, the United States and its citizens have been deeply influenced by the institutions and practices of other countries and the cultures of other peoples.

To make judgments about the role of the United States in the world today and what course American foreign policy should take, citizens need to understand the major elements of international relations and how world affairs affect their own lives and the security and well-being of their communities, states, and nation. They also need to comprehend how commerce, travel, communications, and the international economy bring them into relationships with people everywhere. In elementary and middle schools, students should acquire basic knowledge of the relationship of the United States to other nations and to world affairs. In senior high school, students should develop a more sophisticated understanding of the behaviour of the United States, other nations, and international organisations in the world arena.

Citizenship in American democracy

Citizenship in American constitutional democracy differs from membership in authoritarian or totalitarian regimes. In the United States, each citizen is a full and equal member of a self-governing community and is endowed with fundamental rights and entrusted with responsibilities. Among those responsibilities is seeing that the rights of other individuals are respected. It also is a fundamental responsibility of citizens to see that government serves the purposes for which it was created and that it does not abuse the power that the people have delegated to it.

For instance, the Declaration of Independence proclaims the primary purpose of government: "That to secure these Rights governments are instituted among Men." Further, the Preamble of the U.S. Constitution says that the purposes of government are to "establish Justice, insure domestic Tranquillity, provide for the common defence, promote the general Welfare, and secure the Blessings of Liberty." Citizens are responsible for holding their government accountable to these purposes it was created to serve. Citizens should understand that through their involvement in civic life and in nongovernmental organisations they can help to improve the quality of life in their neighbourhoods, communities, and nation. They also should understand that if they want their voices to be heard, they must become active participants in the political process.

Although elections, campaigns, and voting are at the center of democratic institutions, citizens should be aware that beyond electoral politics there are many other participatory opportunities available to them. Furthermore, the attainment of individual and public goals and participation in political life tend to go hand in hand. The maintenance and improvement of American constitutional democracy is dependent upon the informed, effective, and responsible participation of its citizens.

Intellectual Skills

If citizens are to exercise their rights and discharge their responsibilities as members of self-governing communities, they not only need to acquire a body of knowledge about civic life, politics, and government; they also need to acquire relevant intellectual and participatory skills. Unfortunately, the importance of helping all students develop skills essential for effective and responsible citizenship is not always fully appreciated. Thanks to new research into teaching and learning, however, much more is known about how children develop skills, acquire knowledge, and deepen their understandings. Something we understand now is that learning is "domain specific."

For each subject area, cognitive strategies need to be defined in terms of the concepts of the field. As a result, intellectual skills germane to the field of civics and government, or to the fields of science or mathematics, cannot be learned in isolation. Knowledge of the concepts and the subject matter of civics and government is necessary, for example, to cast an intelligent vote, to understand public issues, or to interact with others to solve public problems. Certain skills in participation are essential and also are specific to the domain of civics and government. Effective and responsible citizenship in a constitutional democracy demands more than knowing and thinking; responsible citizens are expected to participate in the governance of their communities, states, and nation, as well as in the governance of the groups or voluntary associations to which they belong.

Students can and should begin in the earliest grades to acquire the intellectual and participatory skills requisite for informed, effective, and responsible citizenship. They should continue to develop those skills as they proceed through the middle grades and high school.

In this Framework, intellectual skills essential for informed, effective, and responsible citizenship are categorised as identifying and describing, explaining and analysing, and evaluating, taking, and defending positions on public issues. The following items listed below enumerate particular intellectual skills useful to the citizen in comprehending and interpreting civic life.

Identifying and describing

Identifying means to give the meaning or significance of things that are tangible (e.g., such as one's legislative representative) or intangible (e.g., concepts such as justice). To identify something may involve being able to distinguish it from something else; to classify or catalogue something with similar items, or, in some cases, to determine its origin. Describing means to give a verbal or written account of an item's basic attributes or characteristics; describing may refer to tangible or intangible processes, institutions, functions, purposes, or qualities.

- Defining key terms, e.g., constitution, constitutional government, nation-state.
- Making distinctions, e.g., among branches of government, between forms of government, between civil society and the state, between state and local differences in government institutions, legal systems, and jurisdictional forms.

- Identifying individuals, symbols, institutions, e.g., significant civic and political leaders, flags and national monuments, federal and state legislatures.
- Identifying ideas and concepts, e.g., patriotism, majority and minority rights, constitutionalism, civil society, nation-state.
- Identifying emotional language and symbols, e.g., patriot, hawk, dove, flag, Statue of Liberty.
- Describing functions and processes, e.g., legislative checks and balances, judicial review, foreign policy formation.
- Describing historical origins, e.g., of national holidays, sources of democracy, political authority.
- Describing attributes or characteristics, e.g., of local government, American society, systems of shared powers.
- Classifying by attributes, e.g., constitutional democracy, authoritarianism, totalitarianism.
- Describing trends, e.g., participation in politics and civil society, immigration, international influences on American culture.

Explaining and analysing

The following items under the heading "Explaining and Analysing" refer to intellectual skills that also are of importance to the citizen. Explaining means to identify, describe, clarify, or interpret something. One may explain, for example, the causes of events, the meaning or significance of events and ideas, or the reasons for various acts or positions. Analysing means to break something down into its constituent parts in order to clarify its meaning or significance. One may analyse, for example, the causes of events, the components and consequences of ideas, or social, political, or economic processes and institutions.

- Explaining how something works, e.g., electoral system, system of checks and balances, American federal system.
- Analysing reasons for acts, occurrences, and trends, e.g., passage of the 19th amendment, urban riots, voter interest or apathy.
- Explaining the causes and effects of events and phenomena, e.g., creation of the Bill of Rights, election of Franklin D. Roosevelt in 1932, high or low voter turnout.
- Analysing the reasons or motivations for the use of emotional language, e.g., pique public interest, spur action, gain support or sympathy.
- Comparing and contrasting, e.g., limited and unlimited governments, legislative and judicial functions, shared powers and parliamentary systems.
- Distinguishing between opinion and fact, e.g., belief that citizens cannot influence public policy vs. available avenues through which citizens can monitor and influence public policy.
- Distinguishing between means and ends, e.g., between trial by jury and justice, taxation and public safety, foreign aid and national security interests.
- Clarifying responsibilities, e.g., between personal and public responsibilities, between elected officials and citizens.

- Interpreting the meaning or significance of events, ideas, phenomena, e.g., ratification of the Constitution, rule of law, impact of immigration.

Evaluating, taking, and defending positions

Evaluating positions means to use criteria or standards to make judgments about the strengths and weaknesses of positions on issues, goals promoted by the position, or means advocated to attain those goals.

Taking a position refers to using criteria or standards to arrive at a position one can support by selecting from existing positions or creating a novel one.

Defending a position refers to advancing arguments and offering evidence in favour of one's position and responding to or taking into account arguments opposed to one's position.

- Identifying strengths and weaknesses, e.g., of proposed rules, regulations, or legislation.
- Challenging ad hominem and other illogical arguments, e.g., name calling, personal attacks, insinuation and innuendo, circular arguments.
- Evaluating the validity of arguments, analogies, and data, e.g., source of data, omission of data, logical cohesion, circularity of argument, appropriate correspondence of analogies.
- Citing evidence in support or rejection, e.g., reliability of evidence, relevance of evidence, substantiation or contradiction of two or more kinds of evidence.
- Predicting probable consequences, e.g., reliability of predictions, degrees of probability, comparability to past instances.

- Evaluating means and ends, e.g., means not conducive to ends, unethical means and ends, ends that conflict with other desirable ends.
- Assessing the costs and benefits of alternatives, e.g., numbers of people positively or negatively affected, monetary costs vs. societal value.
- Choosing a position from existing alternatives, e.g., analysing existing positions, judging positions using appropriate criteria.
- Creating a novel position, e.g., extracting the best ideas from alternatives, combining elements in unique ways.
- Defending a position, e.g., consistency with fundamental values and principles, costs outweighed by benefits, best and least objectionable among alternatives.
- Responding to opposing arguments, e.g., citing appropriate evidence, countering misstatements or emotive language, pointing out inconsistencies in opposing arguments, accommodating the strengths of different positions, taking into account the best case against one's own position.

Participatory Skills

Participatory skills essential for informed, effective, and responsible citizenship are categorised as interacting, monitoring, and influencing. Education for citizenship must not only address the acquisition of knowledge and intellectual skills; it must also focus on the development of skills required for informed, competent, and responsible participation in the political process and civil society.

The items below refer to various abilities of the citizen to deal effectively with others in political and civic contexts.

Interacting pertains to the skills citizens need to communicate and to work cooperatively with others. To interact is to be responsive to one's fellow citizens. To interact is to question, to answer, and to deliberate with civility, as well as to build coalitions and to manage conflict in a fair, peaceful manner.

Monitoring politics and government refers to the skills citizens need to track the handling of issues by the political process and by government. Monitoring the performance of government and the course of public affairs is essential, if citizens are to participate intelligently.

Influencing refers to the skills required to affect the processes of politics and governance, both formal and informal processes of governance in the community.

1. *Interacting*

 - Working in small groups and committees, pooling information, exchanging opinions, formulating plans of action.
 - Listening, gaining information, ideas, different perspectives.
 - Questioning, clarifying information or points of view, eliciting facts and opinions.
 - Discussing public affairs in a knowledgeable, responsible, and civil manner in school, with neighbours and friends, in community groups and public forums.
 - Participating in voluntary associations and interest groups, promoting ideas, policies, interests.
 - Building coalitions, enlisting the support of like-minded individuals and groups to promote candidates, policies.

- Managing conflicts through mediation, negotiation, compromise, consensus-building, adjudication.
- Performing school and community service, serving as a representative or elected leader, organising a public issues forum, working for one's religious, civic, or charitable organisations.
- Using media resources, obtaining information, exchanging ideas, advocating public policies.
- Deliberating on public issues, e.g., health care, employment, environmental concerns.
- Assessing others' arguments and positions for their validity rather than because of who it is that utters them, remaining calm in the face of opposition.

2. *Monitoring*

- Listening attentively to fellow citizens, proceedings of public bodies, media reports.
- Questioning public officials, experts, and others to elicit information, determine responsibility.
- Holding public officials accountable for using their authority consistently with basic constitutional principles.
- Following public issues in the media, using a variety of sources, such as television, radio, newspapers, journals, and magazines.
- Researching public issues, using computer resources, libraries, the telephone, personal contacts, the media.
- Gathering and analysing information from government officials and agencies, interest groups, civic organisations.

- Attending public meetings and hearings, e.g., student council, city council and school board meetings, briefings by members of county boards of supervisors, state legislatures, and Congress.
- Interviewing people knowledgeable about civic issues, such as local officials, civil servants, experts in public and private associations, members of college and university faculties.
- Using electronic resources for acquiring and exchanging information, e.g., the Internet, online university services, electronic bulletin boards.

3. *Influencing*
   - Voting, e.g., in class, student body, local, state, national, and special elections.
   - Informing, e.g., furnishing factual data to legislators and policymakers.
   - Petitioning, e.g., calling attention of representative bodies and public officials to grievances and desired changes in public policy, gathering signatures for initiatives or recall.
   - Writing, e.g., letters and "op ed" pieces, broadsides, pamphlets.
   - Speaking and testifying before public bodies, e.g., student body councils, school boards, special districts, state legislatures, Congress.
   - Supporting or opposing candidates or positions on public issues, e.g., contributing time, talent, or money.
   - Participating in civic and political groups, e.g., student government, youth groups, local, state, and

national political parties, and ad-hoc advocacy groups.

– Employing the various media to advance points of view on public affairs, e.g., participating in online discussions of public issues, writing newspaper and magazine articles, voicing one's opinion on radio and television talk shows.

Civic Dispositions

Civic dispositions, refers to the traits of private and public character essential to the preservation and improvement of American constitutional democracy. The importance of these civic dispositions can scarcely be overstated. In worrying that the Bill of Rights might be just a "parchment barrier," James Madison wrote that its principles must "acquire by degrees the character of fundamental maxims of free Governments." As Judge Learned Hand put it in our own century, "often wonder whether we do not rest our hopes too much upon constitutions, upon laws and courts. These are false hopes; believe me, these are false hopes. Liberty lies in the hearts of men; when it dies there, no constitution, no law, no court can save it."

Civic dispositions develop slowly over time as a result of what one learns and experiences in the home, school, community, and organisations of civil society. From those experiences should come the understanding that American constitutional democracy requires the responsible self-governance of each individual; one cannot exist without the other. Traits of private character such as moral responsibility, self-discipline, and respect for individual worth and human dignity are essential to the well-being of the American nation, society, and constitutional democracy. Moreover, American constitutional democracy cannot accomplish its purposes, unless its citizens are inclined to participate thoughtfully in public affairs and civic life.

Traits of public character, such as public spiritedness, civility, respect for law, critical mindedness, and a willingness to listen, negotiate, and compromise are indispensable for the nation's well-being. Civic dispositions that contribute to the political efficacy of the individual, the healthy functioning of the political system, a sense of dignity and worth, and the common good include:

– Becoming an independent member of society, e.g., adhering voluntarily to self-imposed standards of behaviour rather than requiring the imposition of external controls, accepting responsibility for the consequences of one's actions, fulfilling the moral and legal obligations of membership in society.

– Assuming the personal, political, and economic responsibilities of a citizen, e.g., taking care of one's self, supporting one's family and caring for, nurturing, and educating one's children, being informed about public issues, serving on juries, voting, paying taxes, performing public service.

– Respecting individual worth and human dignity, e.g., treating everyone with respect, listening to the opinions of others, behaving in a civil manner, considering the rights and interests of others, adhering to the principle of majority rule, respecting the right of the minority to dissent.

– Participating in civic affairs in an informed, thoughtful, and effective manner, e.g., becoming informed prior to voting or participating in public debate, engaging in civic discourse, assuming leadership when appropriate, evaluating whether and when one's obligation as a citizen requires that one's personal desires and interests be subordinated to the public good, and evaluating whether and when moral obligations or constitutional principles require one to reject certain civic expectations.

– Promoting the healthy functioning of American constitutional democracy, e.g., being informed and attentive to public issues, learning about and deliberating on the meaning of constitutional principles, monitoring the adherence of political leaders and governmental agencies to constitutional principles and taking appropriate action if that adherence is lacking, working through peaceful, legal means to change laws that are thought to be unwise or unjust.

Context

Context refers to the arenas in which civic knowledge is acquired, civic skills are employed, and civic dispositions are developed. Contexts in which students learn about civics include the home, school, community, state, nation, and world. These contexts should be taken into account in any assessment of civic knowledge. Learning and applying civic knowledge and skills begins in the home and with early social interaction among friends, relatives, and members of the community. This learning process continues in school as children interact with peers, teachers, school staff members, and administrators to learn about rules, accepted behaviours, and basic democratic and constitutional principles and values. All of these contexts provide a venue in which students can learn about the formal and informal processes of government and civil society.

In the course of their civic education, students should learn that in our federal system, authority and responsibility are divided and shared among local, state, and national governments. Students also should become conversant with systems of governance in other nations as well as with the impact of world affairs on their own lives, communities, and nation. The American political system provides citizens with numerous opportunities for choice and participation. The formal institutions and processes of government such as political parties, campaigns, and elections are important avenues for civic action. Yet equally important avenues are the many associations and groups that constitute civil society, ranging from school clubs to community-based groups to national and international nongovernmental organisations.

The contexts in which students learn about civic life may vary across grade levels. For example, students in the early grades may learn relatively more about civic life, politics, and government from the home and school contexts, while 12th graders may learn relatively more about other nations' political systems and world affairs, because they are more aware of the international context. Similarly, students in the early grades may learn about the informal processes of government by working in small-group situations, while 12th graders may become participants in the more formal institutions of government. Although the home, school, community, and state may receive greater emphasis, national and international contexts should be included.

Political socialisation studies have confirmed repeatedly that young children are more likely to know a national leader than leaders in their state or community. In the United States, most young children are aware that a president is the nation's elected leader and that symbols such as the flag represent their nation. Young children also are aware of major national and international events, thanks to the ubiquitousness of television. In grades 8 and 12, the content should include a broader understanding of the state and nation, as well as of international affairs. At all levels, a balance should be sought between instances involving formal governmental structure and functions and the less formal manifestations of the organisations and relationships, such as voluntary organisations and the family, which constitute civil society.

Home, school, community, state, nation, and world—these are arenas in which students put their knowledge and skills into practice. In the process of utilising their knowledge and skills in these arenas, students not only learn how to monitor and influence public policy; they also deepen their understanding and learn how to interact and participate in a more informed, effective, and responsible manner.

Bibliography

Almond, G*et al.*, *Political Socialization*. Comparative Politics: System, Process andPolicy (Second Edition). Boston: Little, Brown. 1978.

Altbach, P.G., *Higher Education, Democracy, and Development: Implications for NewlyIndustrialized Countries*. Interchange, 1992.

Banks, J.A., *Citizenship Education for a Pluralistic Democratic Society*. Social Studies,1990.

Bastian, A., *Educating for Democracy: Raising Expectations*. NEA Today, 1988.

Berman, E.H., *Civic Education in the Corporatized Classroom*. Theory into Practice,1988.

Beyer, L.E., *Can Schools Further Democratic Practices?* Theory into Practice, 1988.

Boggs, D.L., *Civic Education: An Adult Education Imperative*. Adult EducationQuarterly, 1991.

Boulding, E., *Buiiding a Global Civic Culture: Education for an Interdependent World* .1988, Syracuse: Syracuse University Press.

Bransrn, M.S. *The Education of Citizens in a Market Economy and its Relationship to aFree Society* . in *International Conference on Western Democracy and Eastern Europe: Political,Economic and Social Changes* . 1991.

Butts, R.F. *Democratic Values: What the Schools Should Teach* . in *National Conferenceon the Future of Civic Education* . 1988.

Coleman, J., *Education and Political Development*. Princeton: Princeton UniversityPress.1965

Dahl, R. *The Problem of Civic Competence. Journal of American Democracy*. 1992

Filippov, F.R., *Continuous Education, Democracy and Society.* Soviet Education, 1990.

Finn, C. *Teaching Democracy: Why and How it Must be Taught in a Democratic Society* .in *Nicaraguan Civic Education Conference.* 1991.

Gandal, M. and C. Finn, *Teaching Democracy.* Freedom Papers, 1992.

Gregg, D.R., *Another Viewpoint on Education for Democracy. Social Education,* 1988.

Gutman, A., *Democratic Education in Difficult Times.* Teachers College Record, 1990.

Hepburn, M., *Democratic Education in Schools and Classrooms.* National Council for theSocial Studies Bulletin, 1983.

Ikelov, Orit., *Political Socialization and Schooling Effects Among Israeli Adolescents.*Comparative Education Review, 1991.

Kaltsounis, T., *Democracy and Democratic Citizenship Education.* Social Studies, 1990.

Kamens, D.H., *Education and Democracy: A Comparative and Institutional Analysis.*Sociology of Education, 1988.

Ketcham, R. *A Rationale for Civic Education* in *Annual Meeting of the Social ScienceEducation Consortium.* 1989.

Strike, K.A., *Democracy, Civic Education, and the Problem of Neutrality.* Theory intoPractice, 1988.

Vooglaid, Y. and T. Marja, "Andralogigcal Problems of Building a Democratic Society". *International Journal of Lifelong Education,* 1992.

Index